DEMYSTIFYING BUSINESS DATA VISUALIZATION

Practical Insights into the What and How of Approaching Visualization Projects

DR. M. RAMASUBRAMANIAM & MR. DANIEL PETER

Chennai • Bangalore

CLEVER FOX PUBLISHING
Chennai, India

Published by CLEVER FOX PUBLISHING 2024
Copyright © Dr. M. Ramasubramaniam & Mr.Daniel Peter 2024

All Rights Reserved.
ISBN: 978-93-56486-86-7

This book has been published with all reasonable efforts taken to make the material error-free after the consent of the author. No part of this book shall be used, reproduced in any manner whatsoever without written permission from the author, except in the case of brief quotations embodied in critical articles and reviews.

The Author of this book is solely responsible and liable for its content including but not limited to the views, representations, descriptions, statements, information, opinions and references ["Content"]. The Content of this book shall not constitute or be construed or deemed to reflect the opinion or expression of the Publisher or Editor. Neither the Publisher nor Editor endorse or approve the Content of this book or guarantee the reliability, accuracy or completeness of the Content published herein and do not make any representations or warranties of any kind, express or implied, including but not limited to the implied warranties of merchantability, fitness for a particular purpose. The Publisher and Editor shall not be liable whatsoever for any errors, omissions, whether such errors or omissions result from negligence, accident, or any other cause or claims for loss or damages of any kind, including without limitation, indirect or consequential loss or damage arising out of use, inability to use, or about the reliability, accuracy or sufficiency of the information contained in this book.

FOREWORD

My tryst with data visualization started more than 20 years ago; I was a trainee and was tasked with preparing a report on error and accuracy rates. I used a rudimentary form of MS Excel to convert the tables into a few charts and graphs and could immediately see the difference that visualizations could make. The inferences were able at a glance and users could delve into areas which actually needed attention.

We are now in the middle of one of the biggest revolutions – the AI and information revolution. The world as we knew it has changed and continues to do so at an extremely rapid pace. Data is now abundant and omnipresent. The metric 'time to insight' is used to determine which approach is going to yield actionable knowledge the fastest.

In this age of information overload, the ability to distil complex data into clear, comprehensible visual narratives is more crucial than ever. "Demystifying Business Data Visualization: Practical Insights into the What and How of Approaching Visualization Projects" shines a light on how to navigate your way from data to visualized data and does so with great clarity.

This book is not just about the 'how' of creating visual representations of data; it delves deeper into the 'what' and 'why,' providing a holistic view of the visualization process from conception to execution. It emphasizes the importance of understanding the audience, the message, and the goals of a visualization project, ensuring that the final product is not only aesthetically pleasing but, more importantly, effective in conveying the intended message.

The book's structured approach to understanding visual perception, exploring modern tools, and applying visualization in analytics ensures a comprehensive learning experience. It emphasizes the importance of setting SMART goals, understanding the audience, and selecting the right visualization tools, which are crucial for successful data visualization projects.

This book is designed to assist a wide range of individuals, including data analysts, business intelligence professionals, data scientists, and anyone interested in the field of data visualization. It provides practical insights into the art and science of visualizing data, making it an invaluable resource for those looking to enhance their ability to communicate complex information clearly and effectively.

As you turn the pages of this book, you are embarking on a journey to unlock the power of data visualization in your professional endeavors. Let this book be your guide as you explore the fascinating world of visual data storytelling and may the insights you gain illuminate your path to success.

Mr. Vinay Advani
Director - Artificial Intelligence and
Machine Learning, Cognizant India.

CONTENTS

1. Visualizing Data: Evolution and Pitfalls 1
   Visualizing Data through the Ages: A Journey of Evolution 5
   Changing Landscape: Evolution of IT in Data Visualization 12
   Avoiding the Pitfalls: Overcoming Challenges of Poor
   Visualization 19
2. Understanding Visual Perception 28
   The Wonders of the Human Eye 28
   Unveiling the Gestalt Principles 30
   Building Blocks for Effective Data Visualization 36
   Exploring Data: A Comprehensive Guide 37
   Unraveling Semantic Attributes in Visualization 40
   Choosing the Right Visual: Making Informed Decisions 55
   Captivating Your Audience: Visualization with Audience
   in Mind 57
   Exercises 58
3. Harnessing the Power of Visualization in Analytics 59
   Exploratory Analysis: Unveiling Insights through Visualization .. 59
   Visualizations for Effective Exploratory Analysis 61
   Driving Success with SMART Goals in Data Visualization 67
   Unleashing the Potential of Visualizing Categorical Data 70
   Exercises 76

4. Navigating the Visualization Project – Steps and Considerations 78

Business Scoping: Defining the Project Scope 79

Stages in Business Scoping: A Roadmap for Successful Projects . 81

Data Sources: Understanding and Selecting Relevant Data 82

Data Acquisition: Collecting and Preparing Data for Visualization. 90

Defining Business Logic from Data 92

Audience Focus: Tailoring Visualization for Effective Communication 96

Exercise 100

5. Exploring Modern Tools for Data Visualization 104

Factors Influencing Tool Selection: Considerations 105

Tools Available in the Market: Overview of Visualization Tool Options 112

Self-Service Data Visualization: Empowering with User-Friendly Tools 117

Exercise 120

CASE STUDY: Unveiling Insights from Music Sales Data with GenerativeAI's Guidance *123*

Objective 123

Scenario 123

Enhancing Learning: Unlocking the Power of GenerativeAI 124

Chapter Integration 124

Steps 125

Conclusion 129

Additional Resources 130

Conclusion *131*

References *133*

FIGURES

Figure 1: Call Flow Between Locations 5
Figure 2: First Known Pie Chart William Playfair 1801 6
Figure 3: Playfair's trade-balance time-series chart, published in his Commercial and Political Atlas, 1786 7
Figure 4: Napolean's march to Russia 8
Figure 5: BigData Expo In China 9
Figure 6: Petrol Pumps In Google Map 10
Figure 7: Bigdata Conference In China 11
Figure 8: Evolution of Information Technology -- Visualization Perspective 13
Figure 9: Tesla Car Dashboard 15
Figure 10: Time series Decomposition 18
Figure 11: Burden Of Debt 20
Figure 12: Rising Tide 22
Figure 13: Consumer Sentiments Index 24
Figure 14: World Political Map 26
Figure 15: How Human Brain Processes & Preceives Information 29
Figure 16: Laws Of Similarity 31
Figure 17: GDP Per Capita Vs Self-reported Life Satisfaction 31
Figure 18: Trends In Life Satisfaction 33
Figure 19: Urban Vs Rural Employment By Sector 35
Figure 20: Life Expectancy Vs Income 37
Figure 21: Superstore's Super Sankey 38
Figure 22: Screenshot From Tableau 40
Figure 23: Sample Dashboard - Specificity 42
Figure 24: Column Chart With Size 44

Figure 25: World GDP Map 45
Figure 26: Foreign Currency World Map.. 45
Figure 27: CO2 Emissions Per Capita 47
Figure 28: Cluster Analysis... 47
Figure 29: Skype Emoticons 49
Figure 30: Twitter Emoji 50
Figure 31: Dashboard Sample Klipfolio.. 51
Figure 32: Dashboard Sample Hootsuite 51
Figure 33: Bubble Chart.. 53
Figure 34: Telecom Data Reconciliation KPI 56
Figure 35: Box Plot - Rate Plan 63
Figure 36: Combo Chart - Amount Spent... 64
Figure 37: Combo Chart - Garment Rejection Analysis 64
Figure 38: Word Cloud - Sentiment Analysis... 66
Figure 39: SMART Goal 70
Figure 40: Connected Scatter Plot 74
Figure 41: Parallel Coordinate Plot... 75
Figure 42: Fixed Length Binary 84
Figure 43: ASN.1 85
Figure 44: Text File 86
Figure 45: JSON 87
Figure 46: Still Image 87
Figure 47: Colors... 88
Figure 48: Mapview Data 89
Figure 49: Map.. 89
Figure 50: OCR 90
Figure 51: Visualization Process Flow 92
Figure 52: Subscription Table Schema Sample...................................... 93
Figure 53: Car Dashboard 98
Figure 54: Architecture.. 109

TABLES

Table 1: Goss Debt (Rs Cr/ Firm Inflation adjusted) figures 21
Table 2: Reference Table for Color 71
Table 3: Data Dictionary 71
Table 4: Summary Output Before Transformation 72
Table 5: Summary Output Transformed 72
Table 6: Erroneous 73
Table 7: Hosting In-house Vs Cloud 106
Table 8: TCO Calculator 112

CHAPTER 1

VISUALIZING DATA: EVOLUTION AND PITFALLS

*A*s you embark on this journey through the pages of this book, we find ourselves in truly fascinating times. Not only are we witnessing the remarkable growth of economies worldwide, but there is an underlying force driving this transformative change. A force that was inconceivable just a few decades ago. It is awe-inspiring to reflect on the past decade and the apprehension that gripped the world as we approached the turn of the millennium. The infamous "Y2K" problem, also known as the millennium bug, was surrounded by much anticipation. Yet, as January 1, 2000, dawned upon us, the transition was seamless, and the fears of computerized financial chaos proved unfounded. We can vividly remember how smoothly the dates rolled over, with only minor glitches reported across the globe.

Now, let us fast forward to the present decade, where we find ourselves amidst the fourth Industrial Revolution. This era is marked by reduced human intervention and an increased reliance on automated manufacturing processes. Smart, interconnected technologies and Artificial Intelligence are reshaping the entire lifecycle of parts and products, from design and production to usage and maintenance. By embracing this digital reality, organizations and individuals alike are experiencing profound transformations. Klaus Schwab, a prominent figure, considers this the Information Age, powered by the remarkable advances in data science. It stands as a significant milestone in the progression of human civilization, following the steam power and mechanized production of the 19th century, followed by electricity's role in enabling mass production and the subsequent automation brought by electronics and information technology. We can now anticipate a future of high-end automation and markets gravitating towards perfect competition.

Within management circles, it is widely debated that crucial decisions are often driven more by experience and intuition rather than rational, scientific, data-driven inputs. However, informed decisions necessitate access to relevant information and knowledge. The foundation of knowledge is built upon insights, which, in turn, are empowered by data. Hence, it holds true that data-driven decision-making is essential for making informed choices. This is precisely where the significance of data visualization becomes apparent, opening doors to remarkable opportunities.

Data visualization plays a pivotal role in business analytics and decision-making. It is of paramount importance to understand the fundamental concepts of visualizing business data and effectively communicating insights through various visual forms, especially for those with an interest in analytics and decision science. As a field, data visualization encompasses a wide range of disciplines, including psychology, cognitive sciences, and artistic expression. Consequently, it offers an intriguing and dynamic field of study that captivates the interest of individuals from all backgrounds.

As you immerse yourself in the contents of this book, we hope to guide you through the captivating world of data visualization, equipping you with the knowledge and skills to navigate this ever-evolving landscape. Together, we will explore the art and science of transforming complex data into compelling visuals that enable effective communication and decision-making. So, let us embark on this exhilarating journey, and embrace the power of data visualization in shaping our understanding of the world around us.

Let's begin by formally defining the term "Data Visualization." In this book, we define data visualization as a "visual representation of historical and predictive information, whether quantitative or qualitative." Its purpose is to effectively communicate, explore, analyze, and discover insights within small or large datasets using appropriate visual tools for reporting purposes.

It is also important for readers to understand what data visualization is not, as outlined in this book. We intentionally exclude the "fancy" world of "Infographics" from our definition of data visualization. Infographics often straddle the line between exploration and communication, presenting loosely connected graphs, charts, or pictures. Their meaning may be known only to the designer, and they typically serve marketing communication purposes. In contrast, the visuals presented in this textbook are designed to allow users to explore and gain an understanding of the data. Additionally, dashboards, which will be discussed in future chapters, differ from infographics. Dashboards provide users with the ability to delve deeper into the data and answer intriguing questions.

It is crucial to acknowledge that data visualization aims to be truthful and unbiased. Unlike infographics, which may present a captivating story but fail to convey accurate information, data visualization is meant to provide truthful representations of data.

Data visualization can also be viewed as an abstract concept where different points, areas, and volumes are employed to represent data. In modern visualizations, we now have networks that illustrate relationships between social media interactions. Maps, such as choropleth maps, are also a part of data visualization, conveying generic information about the data.

By understanding the essence of data visualization and its various forms, we can dive into the captivating world of visualizing data and gain valuable insights. Throughout this book, we will explore different techniques and approaches that empower individuals to effectively communicate and make informed decisions based on data. So, let us embrace this journey and unlock the power of data visualization together.

Visualization can be seen as an abstract concept where data is represented using different points, areas, and volumes. Nowadays, visualization goes beyond traditional forms and includes "networks" that illustrate relationships between social media interactions. It also encompasses maps like choropleth maps, which convey generic information about the data. To better understand this concept, let us consider the diagram below. It showcases the call flow between locations, with the color scale indicating the number of calls within a specific time range. This serves as a compelling example of visualizing networks and how data can be effectively communicated through visualization techniques.

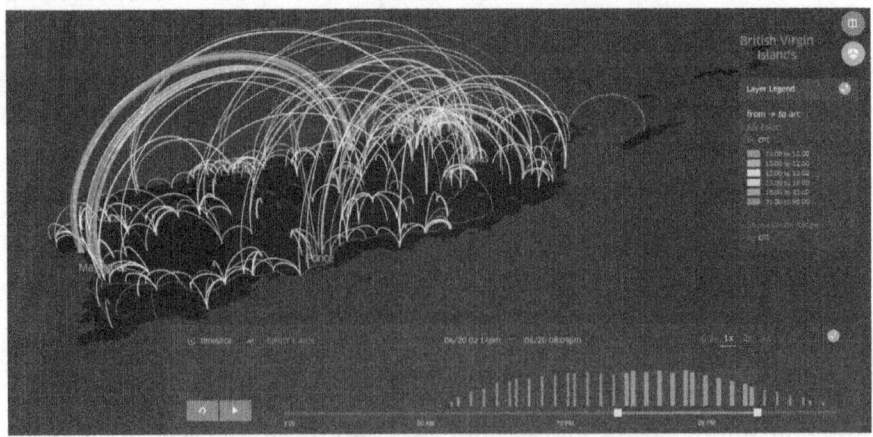

Figure 1: Call Flow Between Locations

Visualizing Data through the Ages: A Journey of Evolution

In addition to gaining a solid understanding of what data visualization entails, it is also intriguing to explore its evolution over time. Numerous individuals have contributed to this field, including anthropologists seeking to uncover artifacts. Notable figures such as William Playfair, John W. Tuckey, Jacques Bertin, Edward Tufte, and Michael Friendly have made significant contributions to the history of data visualization. Michael Friendly, in particular, has done an exceptional job summarizing this work and providing a captivating introduction to the subject's history in his book *Handbook of Data Visualization*.

According to Friendly, the evolution of data visualization has progressed through various phases. In the earlier stages, the focus was primarily on maps and diagrams representing geographical locations. The second phase centered around measurement and theory, exploring new ways to represent data. It was during the 1800s that we witnessed the birth of modern visualization, marked by the evaluation and introduction of new graphic forms. However, the field experienced a lull during the late 1800s to the late 1900s.

Fortunately, there was a resurgence of interest in visualization during the late 1900s, leading us to the present day, where we now can visualize high-dimensional data and even employ holograms in the process. Now, let us delve into some fascinating examples of evolutionary data visualizations.

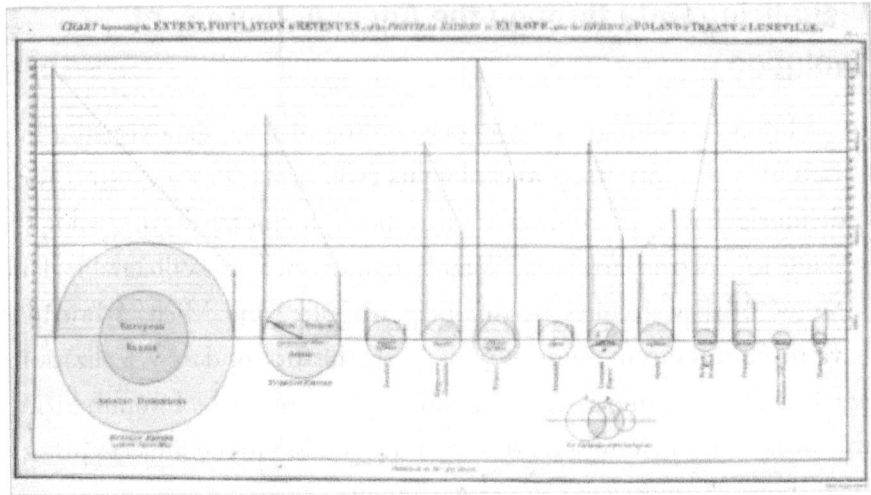

Figure 2: First Known Pie Chart William Playfair 1801

(Source: A version of this article appears in print on April 22, 2012, on Page MM34 of the Sunday Magazine with the headline: Who Made That? (Pie Chart).)

William Playfair, a trained practical engineer during the Industrial Revolution, holds the distinction of being considered the founder of graphical methods of statistics. He made significant contributions to data visualization, including the invention of several types of graphical representations, one of which is the pie chart. The provided pie chart is from Playfair's "Statistical Breviary," a publication containing statistical data of European countries dating back to 1801. This pie chart is recognized as the first known instance of a pie chart. Playfair had a deep understanding of the psychological needs of readers and aimed to provide graphics that were easy to interpret.

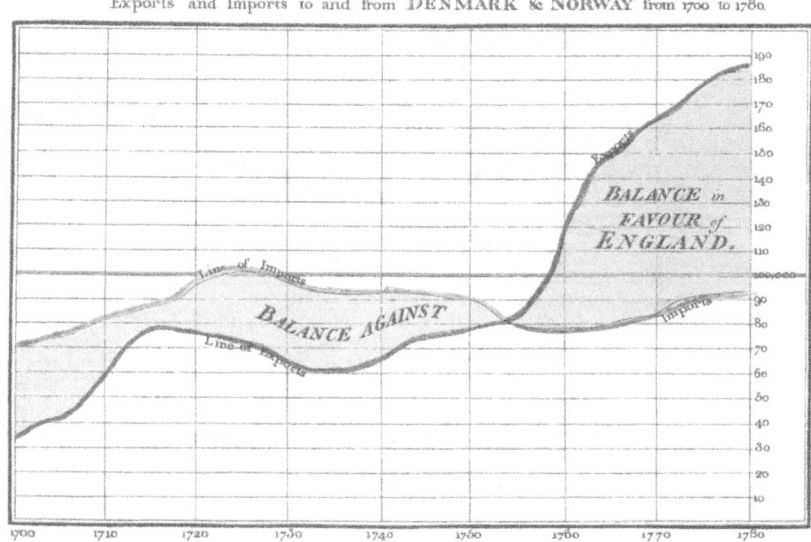

Figure 3: Playfair's trade-balance time-series chart, published in his
Commercial and Political Atlas, 1786
(Source: Playfair's Commercial and Political Atlas of 1786)

During a time when tables were commonly used for presenting statistical information, William Playfair introduced the line chart as an alternative method. He emphasized the significance of interactions between lines in conveying information effectively. While some of the charts attributed to him may not be entirely his original work, Playfair made substantial contributions to the design ideas of data visualization.

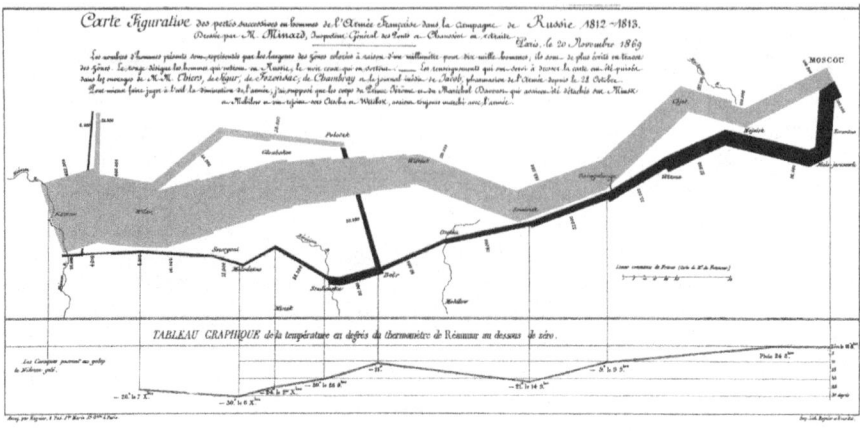

Figure 4: Napolean's march to Russia
(Source: DataVizBlog)

One of the timeless classics in data visualization is Joseph Minard's depiction of Napoleon's failed campaign. This visualization tells a compelling story of the Grand Army, starting with 442,000 soldiers and gradually dwindling to only 10,000 upon their return. Minard skillfully combines various elements such as demographics, time, temperature, and the direction of the army's movement. The striking feature of this visualization is the representation of the army's size using golden and black bands, with each millimeter on the chart equivalent to 10,000 men.

Major battles, geographical landmarks, and the harsh temperatures encountered during river crossings are also marked. In 1871, after Minard's passing, his obituary praised his graphical innovations, stating that he replaced dry and complex statistical columns with visually intuitive images that could be understood at a glance, eliminating mental fatigue and immediately conveying natural consequences and unforeseen comparisons.

Unleashing the Power of Modern Data Visualization

In today's modern era, data visualizations have taken on a whole new level of sophistication. The advancements made in this field are truly awe-inspiring. A striking example of this progress can be seen in the picture captured at a Big Data Expo in China. The image showcases a mesmerizing 3D visualization of a Smart City, which serves as a testament to how far we have come in the realm of data visualization.

But the advancements do not stop there. We are witnessing the integration of technologies like Virtual Reality and Augmented Reality into business data visuals, revolutionizing decision science across various industries. These immersive technologies are opening up endless possibilities for exploring and understanding data, offering insights and solutions to every imaginable use case. The future of data visualization holds incredible potential, with constant innovation and groundbreaking techniques paving the way for even more captivating and informative visual representations of complex data. As technology continues to evolve, we can only imagine the breathtaking visualizations that lie ahead, transforming the way we perceive and interact with information.

Figure 5: BigData Expo In China

In the present day, there are ongoing projects that aim to capture street views at regular intervals using satellite imagery. These projects utilize image recognition technology to analyze the data and extract valuable insights. For example, they can track the number of trees in a specific geographic area over time or monitor the growth of vehicle traffic. Additionally, platforms like Google Maps offer statistics and visual representations of various amenities, such as restaurants or schools, in a given location.

To illustrate this, the image below showcases the visual representation of available petrol pumps in the Nungambakkam area of Chennai, India. This visualization provides a clear and informative overview of the distribution and density of petrol pumps in that specific locality.

Figure 6: Petrol Pumps In Google Map

These advancements in data visualization and analytics empower us to gain a deeper understanding of our surroundings, enabling better decision-making and resource allocation. By harnessing the power of technology and data, we can uncover valuable insights that contribute to the development and improvement of our communities.

The size of data visualizations has indeed evolved to cater to different display formats, ranging from smartphone screens as small as 4 inches to computer screens measuring 14 inches and even larger LED displays spanning several feet. The image below showcases an impressive example of a 10 x 14 feet dashboard displayed in a conference hall. This large-scale visualization allows for the clear and comprehensive presentation of data, ensuring visibility and impact for the audience.

Figure 7: BIGDATA CONFERENCE IN CHINA

Moreover, in the modern era, user experience (UX) design plays a crucial role in data visualization. UX design focuses on creating intuitive, user-friendly interfaces that enhance the overall experience of interacting with visualized data. By incorporating principles of usability, accessibility, and aesthetics, UX design ensures that data visualizations are not only informative but also engaging and easy to comprehend.

As technology continues to advance, we can anticipate further innovations in data visualization, accommodating diverse display sizes and incorporating sophisticated UX design principles. These advancements will enable users to derive meaningful insights from data across various platforms and environments, promoting effective communication and decision-making.

Changing Landscape: Evolution of IT in Data Visualization

The evolution of Information Technology (IT) from a data visualization perspective has been remarkable. Visualization software has made significant progress, becoming a vital component in the field of IT. The visualization layer serves as the face of any software, and its quality has become a key factor in the success of IT solutions. Even if the core components of the software are advanced, poor visualization can hinder its pre-sales process.

In addition to user interface (UI) developers, UX (User Experience) designers have emerged as crucial contributors to software development. Their expertise in creating intuitive and user-friendly interfaces has become invaluable. The collaboration between UI developers and UX designers has led to the improvement of data visualization in software applications. The infographic below provides a summarized overview of the evolution of Information Technology from a data visualization perspective:

Visualizing Data: Evolution and Pitfalls

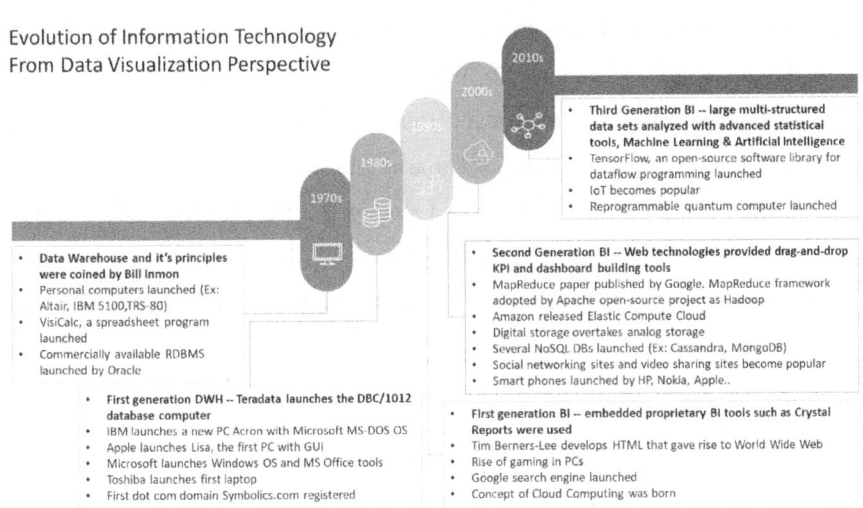

Figure 8: Evolution of Information Technology -- Visualization Perspective

The field of data visualization has witnessed significant advancements in the past few decades, aligning with the progress in Information Technology (IT). Here are some key milestones and developments that have shaped data visualization from the 1970s to the present:

- 1970s:
  - Introduction of the concept of Data Warehouses by William H. Inmon.
  - Emergence of personal computers, although not widely available for general consumers.
  - Launch of VisiCalc, the first computerized spreadsheet, providing improved reporting capabilities.
  - Commercial release of Oracle, a widely used Relational Database Management System (RDBMS).
- 1980s:
  - Teradata introduces specialized database computers, paving the way for large-scale data warehousing.

- Bill Inmon publishes influential books on Data Warehouse design.
- Launch of IBM's PC with MS-DOS, popularizing the term "PC."
- Introduction of graphical user interfaces (GUI) on personal computers, such as Apple Lisa and Macintosh.
- Microsoft launches Windows OS and its popular MS Office tools.
- Introduction of compact laptops by Toshiba.
- Registration of the first .com domain, symbolics.com, marking the beginning of the World Wide Web.

- 1990s:
  - Founding of Prism Solutions by Bill Inmon, offering data warehousing solutions.
  - Embedded proprietary Business Intelligence (BI) tools, including Crystal Reports.
  - HTML is published, giving shape to the World Wide Web.
  - Rise of PC gaming.
  - Development of Google search engine.
  - Birth of the concept of Cloud Computing.
  - Internet usage for communication and entertainment purposes.
  - Proliferation of computer training institutes.

- 2000s:
  - Web technologies enable drag-and-drop KPI and dashboard-building tools.
  - Google publishes the MapReduce paper, leading to the adoption of the Hadoop framework for Big Data processing.
  - Amazon releases Elastic Compute Cloud (EC2), triggering discussions about centralized computing power.
  - Digital storage surpasses analog storage media.
  - Launch of several NoSQL databases (e.g., Cassandra, MongoDB).
  - Emergence of popular social networking and video-sharing platforms.

- Introduction of smartphones by various companies, leading to the development of visual-oriented mobile apps.
- 2010s:
  - Third-generation BI with real-time predictive analytics and artificial intelligence.
  - Enhanced data visualization capabilities with multiple dimensions and faster drill-downs.
  - Rise of image recognition and video analytics for advanced data visualization.
  - Implementation of advanced visualization in driverless vehicles, such as Tesla cars.
  - The Tesla car dashboard serves as an example of real-time statistics and image recognition analytics in modern data visualization applications.

Figure 9: Tesla Car Dashboard

- 2020 onwards:
  - Continued growth of Artificial Intelligence (AI) and Machine Learning (ML): AI and ML technologies are expected to advance further in the 2020s, enabling more sophisticated data visualization

techniques. AI-driven insights and automated data visualization processes may become more prevalent.

- Increased focus on interactive and immersive visualizations: With the availability of technologies like virtual reality (VR) and augmented reality (AR), there may be a shift towards interactive and immersive data visualizations that provide users with a more engaging and intuitive experience.
- Integration of data visualization with the Internet of Things (IoT): As the number of connected devices and sensors increases, there will be opportunities to visualize real-time data from IoT networks. This can lead to new visualization techniques and insights for industries such as smart cities, healthcare, and manufacturing.
- Enhanced accessibility and inclusivity: Efforts will likely continue to make data visualization accessible to a wider audience, including individuals with disabilities. This may involve the development of accessible visualization tools, adherence to accessibility guidelines, and consideration of diverse user needs.
- Ethical considerations in data visualization: As data privacy and ethics gain more attention, there may be a greater emphasis on responsible data visualization practices. This includes ensuring transparency, avoiding biased representations, and respecting user consent and privacy.
- Integration of data storytelling: Data storytelling combines narrative elements with visualizations to effectively communicate insights and engage audiences. In the 2020s, there may be an increased focus on the integration of storytelling techniques into data visualization to create compelling narratives and drive understanding.
- Advancements in data visualization tools and platforms: Technology companies and developers will likely continue to innovate and improve data visualization tools, making them more user-friendly, versatile, and powerful. This can include advancements in data visualization libraries, software, and cloud-based platforms.

Overall, the evolution of IT has greatly influenced the progress of data visualization, from the early days of basic visuals to the current era of advanced analytics and AI-driven insights.

Throughout the evolution of Information Technology, several noteworthy developments have shaped the field of data visualization. In its early stages, software was primarily used for summarization and calculations. However, the introduction of operating systems like Apple's Macintosh and Microsoft's Windows brought prominence to the presentation layer, leading to progress in visualization techniques.

The cost of processing power decreased over time, and the advent of Cloud computing revolutionized data processing and visualization by reducing upfront investments. This era of Information Technology also witnessed the development of various software tools for data acquisition, communication, monitoring, auditing, network management, deployment stack, coordination, storage, and computation, all of which paved the way for advanced data visualization capabilities.

Computers evolved from handling unstructured data and flat files to embracing Relational Database Management Systems (RDBMS), enabling online transaction processing and online analytics with features like multidimensional cubes. Later, the emergence of big data technologies, such as columnar and in-memory data processing, allowed for data summarization before loading it into databases, enabling analytics and visualizations directly from unstructured data. The increased processing power, thanks to low-cost RAM, modern CPUs and GPUs, and high-resolution displays, facilitated the development of advanced graphical cards that support multi-screen displays. The combination of UX design and UI development contributed to interactive visualizations, ultimately giving rise to the popular technology we know today as Data Visualization.

Microsoft's provision of Excel and PowerPoint deserves acknowledgment for making data visualization accessible to all computer users. The ability to create charts with a simple click within a spreadsheet table was subsequently adopted by several Business Intelligence (BI) software providers for visualization purposes.

Furthermore, the field of data visualization has been empowered by the statistical theories developed over centuries, enabling visual modeling and visual queries. Business users can now perform descriptive, exploratory, and advanced predictive analytics using visual means. Interactive and dynamic data visualization techniques have added an extra layer of interest and engagement to the field. Below is an example of time-series decomposition and forecasting.

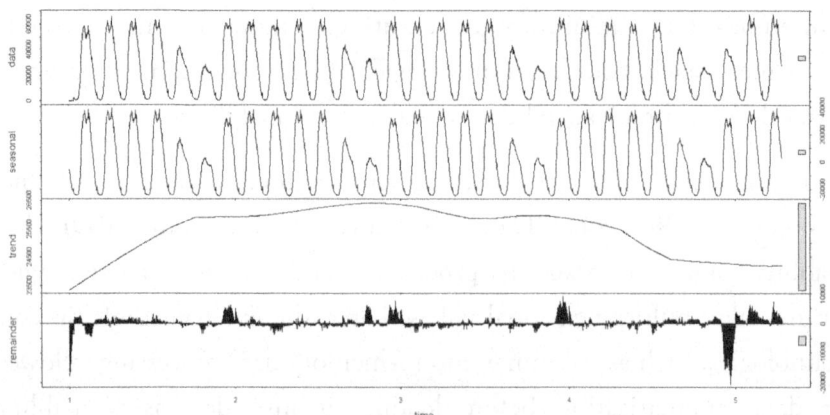

Figure 10: Time series Decomposition

In summary, the evolution of Information Technology has profoundly influenced data visualization, transitioning it from basic summarization to a sophisticated discipline capable of handling massive amounts of complex data structures.

Avoiding the Pitfalls: Overcoming Challenges of Poor Visualization

In addition to understanding good visualization principles, it is also important to train our eyes to recognize bad visuals. A visualization expert can easily identify the flaws in poorly designed graphs or charts. That is why we have dedicated a section for beginners who want to learn how to identify and understand the reasons behind poor visualizations, often referring to Tufte's principles. The intention is not to criticize those who created these graphs and charts but rather to provide valuable insights on what not to do when designing visualizations, which is crucial in our perspective.

Case 1: The Burden of Debt

Debt is a crucial financial metric for assessing a firm's long-term stability and leverage. Gross debt refers to the total amount of debt obligations a company has, including both long-term and short-term borrowings. Ideally, gross debt should be controlled relative to other financial parameters, although it may increase if the company is expanding its business.

The purpose of the following graph is to illustrate the disproportionate increase in Gross Debt under stress (Rs. Cr) since 2007. The graph also includes the number of stressed firms as a reference on a dual axis.

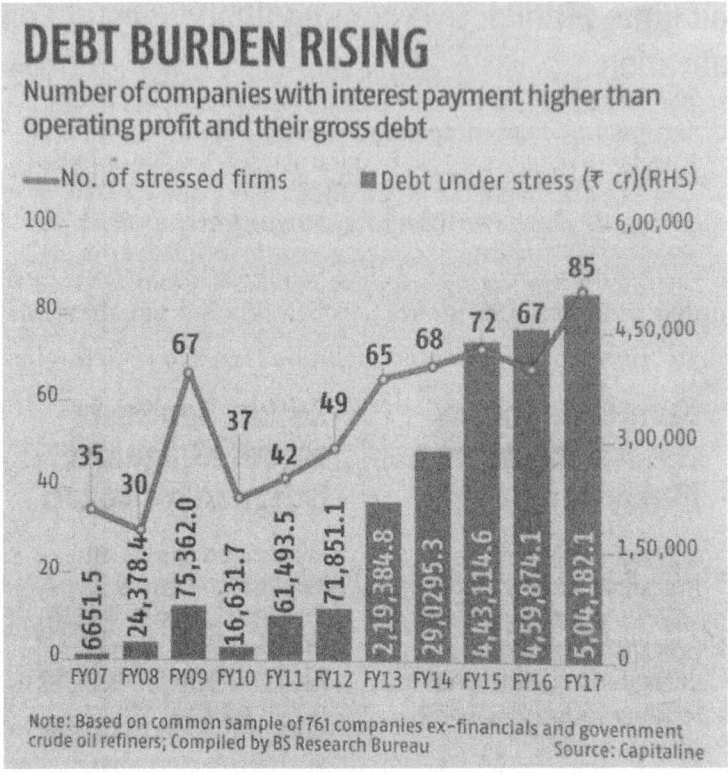

Figure 11: Burden Of Debt
(Source: Capitaline)

However, there is a design issue with this chart due to the use of a dual axis. A design variation refers to any variation that distorts the data. In this case, using different scales to represent the number of firms and their gross debt introduces data distortion. For example, one unit on the left side of the Y-axis represents 20 firms, while one unit on the right side represents 1,50,000 Rs. By presenting both variables together, the designer implies a relationship between the number of indebted firms and the gross debt. Unless this association is scientifically proven, it is better to avoid using such graphs.

We applied Tufte's lie factor calculation to analyze this graph. As per Tufte's principle, monetary values should represent real values. To account for inflation, we considered the base year as 2007. Additionally, since the sample size varies over time, it is more appropriate to calculate the gross debt per firm instead of considering all the firms. The results of the lie factor calculation are presented in the table below:

Table 1: Goss Debt (Rs Cr/ Firm Inflation adjusted) figures

YEAR	Debt	NUMBER OF DEBT FIRMS	CPI	DEBT PER FIRM (ADJUSTED FOR INFLATION)
FY07	6651.5	35	1	190.04
FY08	24378.4	30	1.003	810.18
FY09	75362	67	1.007	1116.98
FY10	16631.7	37	1.01	445.05
FY11	61493.5	42	1.013	1445.34
FY12	71851.1	49	1.017	1441.83
FY13	219384.8	65	1.02	3308.97
FY14	290295.3	68	1.023	4173.06
FY15	443114.6	72	1.027	5992.57
FY16	459874.1	67	1.03	6663.87
FY17	504182	85	1.033	5742.06
	% Change Adjusted Value	**29.21**		
	% Change unadjusted Value	**74.79**		

Upon analyzing the data, it becomes evident that the graph inaccurately represents the increase in Debt under stress. The graph falsely portrays a 75% increase, whereas the actual increase is only 29%. This results in a lie factor of approximately 3, which indicates a significant distortion of the data. Ideally, the lie factor should be close to 1, reflecting a faithful representation of reality.

Case 2: Corporate Bonds Issued (Rs Cr)

In the world of financial graphs presented in newspapers, it is crucial for readers to be knowledgeable enough to differentiate between accurate and distorted information. Here, we have an example of a graph that falls into the latter category. This particular graph was published in a prominent financial newspaper and exhibits both design and data variations. One noticeable inconsistency is the placement of the year 2016-17 right in the middle of 2013-14 and 2014-15. This order inconsistency creates confusion for the readers.

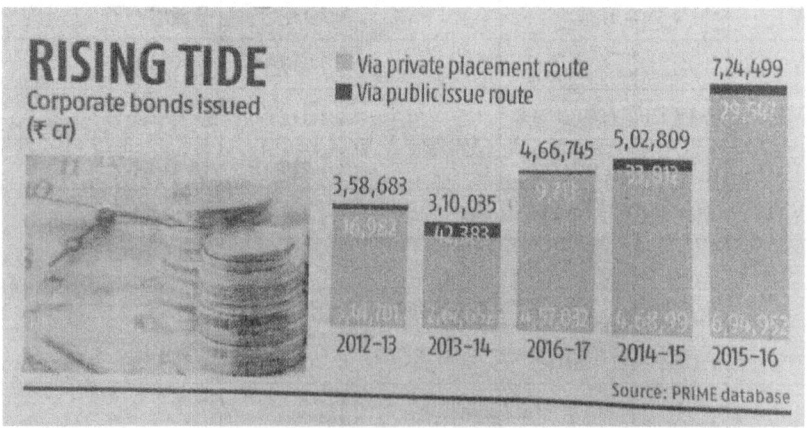

Figure 12: Rising Tide
(Source: PRIME database)

Furthermore, instead of presenting the two categories of placement route value and public issue value side by side, the newspaper has superimposed them. This design choice adds even more complexity to the graph. Additionally, it takes some time to realize that the value of 16,982 represents the difference between 358,683 and 341,701. Introducing a third number unrelated to the original set of units further confuses the audience rather than providing them with clear information. Another important aspect to note is that the monetary values in the graph are not adjusted for CPI (Consumer Price Index), which means inflation is not taken into account.

Overall, this graph fails to accurately present the data due to the order inconsistency, superimposed categories, introduction of unrelated numbers, and the lack of adjustment for inflation. It serves as a reminder for readers to critically analyze and question the graphs presented in financial publications.

Case 3: The (Inflated) Consumer Sentiment Index

Newspapers have a tendency to perpetuate economic fallacies, and one such example is the Consumer Sentiment Index. This index is commonly used to assess the overall state of the economy. However, it is important to recognize that the index is based on the perceptions of a selected sample of individuals from diverse geographic regions, reflecting their opinions about the state of the economy. Here is a graph depicting the Consumer Sentiment Index:

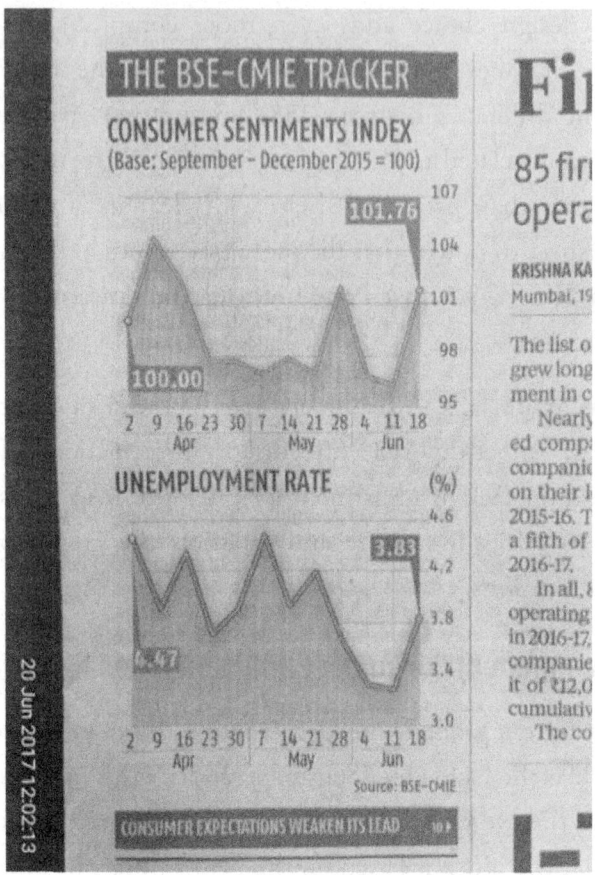

Figure 13: Consumer Sentiments Index

The first question that often arises is whether there is a relationship between the Consumer Sentiment Index (CSI) and the unemployment rate. To explore this further, let's take a closer look at how the CSI is calculated by the BSE Sentiment Index. The calculation involves conducting a survey among people, focusing on five different aspects of their daily economic and financial lives. The survey includes the following questions and answer choices:

- Question 1: How is your family faring financially these days compared to a year ago?

- Question 2: How do you think your family will be faring financially a year from now?
- Question 3: How would you describe the financial and business conditions in our country for the next 12 months?
- Question 4: What do you think the financial and business conditions in our country will be like for the next five years?
- Question 5: Do you think this is generally a good or bad time to make purchases like furniture, refrigerators, televisions, two-wheelers, and cars?

It is important to note that the calculation of the CSI does not involve the use of the unemployment rate. Instead, it focuses on capturing people's perceptions and opinions. Therefore, the graph distorts the data by presenting a design variation, where the unemployment rate graph is placed directly below the CSI graph. In statistical terms, this represents a "spurious relationship." While we acknowledge that there may be some association between the variables in general, it is better to avoid presenting such graphs.

When examining the relationship between the CSI and the unemployment rate or any other economic indicators, it is crucial to consider the methodology and data sources used. Understanding that the CSI reflects people's perceptions rather than objective economic data can help us interpret it appropriately. Additionally, it is advisable to analyze multiple indicators and economic data points to gain a more comprehensive understanding of the state of the economy.

Case 4: Bias in the land measurement

We are all familiar with the world political map, that gives us a general understanding of the different continents and countries around the globe. However, it is important to note that the map we commonly encounter is subject to a bias in land measurement. Specifically, countries that are closer to the northern and southern hemispheres appear smaller than they are when compared to countries located near the equator. This bias can be observed in the traditional world map that we have been exposed to since our primary school days. The image below depicts this commonly used world map:

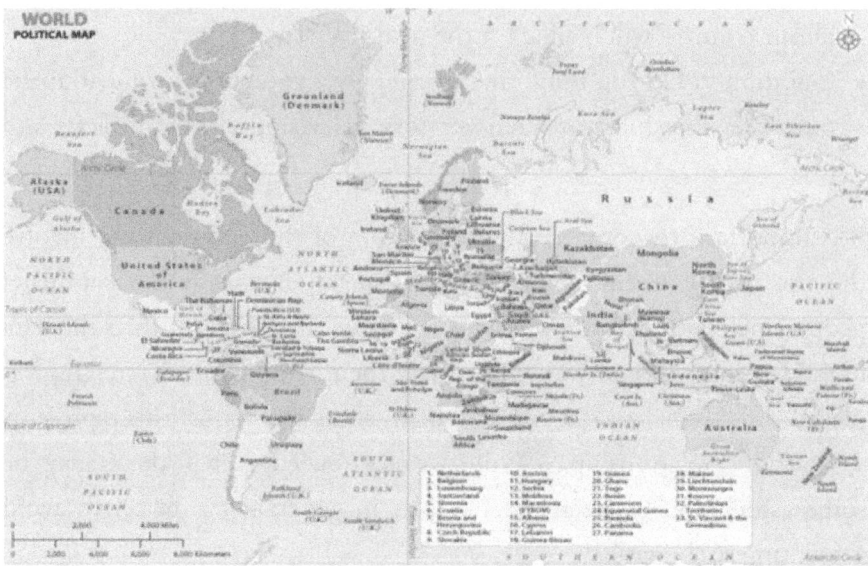

Figure 14: World Political Map

When examining the map provided above, it is evident that Africa (the continent) and Greenland (a province within the country of Denmark) appear to be similar in size. However, this visual representation is deceptive, as the reality is quite different. Africa is approximately 14 times larger than Greenland. Africa spans an area of around 30.37 million square kilometers, whereas Greenland covers an area of 2.166 million square kilometers. This stark contrast in size is not accurately reflected on the map.

Another example worth considering is the comparison between Greenland and India. On the map, India may appear significantly smaller than Greenland, giving the impression that Greenland is much larger.

However, in reality, Greenland is smaller than India, accounting for approximately two-thirds of India's size.

The distortion in size that occurs on flat maps is significant and can mislead viewers. This highlights the importance of being cautious when selecting maps to represent key performance indicators (KPIs) and other geospatial data in data visualization. Geospatial analytics and the use of maps in data visualization play a vital role in today's context. Therefore, it is crucial to choose the appropriate map projection or representation that accurately reflects the sizes and proportions of geographical areas, avoiding deceptive visual distortions.

By being mindful of the limitations of flat maps and employing suitable techniques in geospatial analytics, we can ensure that the maps we use provide an accurate and informative portrayal of geographical data. This allows us to make informed decisions and gain valuable insights from geospatial analysis.

In summary:

- Insights derived from data play a crucial role in making effective decisions.
- Data visualization is a powerful tool for facilitating efficient and informed decision-making processes.
- Data visualization draws upon principles from various disciplines, including psychology, arts, and science, to effectively communicate information.
- The field of data visualization has evolved over time, incorporating advancements in technology and design.
- It's important to recognize that data can be misrepresented or manipulated, and charts can be misleading. Therefore, careful chart design or understanding of charts created by others is essential to ensure accurate interpretation and avoid misinterpretation.

CHAPTER 2

UNDERSTANDING VISUAL PERCEPTION

*D*espite the advancements in Artificial Intelligence and Machine Learning, it is fascinating to acknowledge that the human mind still surpasses a mere number-crunching machine. While our brains may not match the computational speed of these machines, they excel at what they do best. Similar to a machine, our brains take in information, process it, and generate outputs. However, it is important to recognize that the human brain does not interpret inputs in the exact way they were presented. Understanding this intricate process requires delving into the realm of Optometry 101. Fortunately, since our goal is to comprehend the underlying phenomenon rather than approaching it from an ophthalmologist's perspective, let's explore how the brain processes and perceives information.

The Wonders of the Human Eye

Imagine you're strolling along a forest trail when suddenly you hear a nearby roar. Your instinct prompts you to look in that direction, and there it is—a tiger. In a fraction of a second, your brain switches into flight mode rather than fight mode. So much happens in this moment; let's look at the below figure:

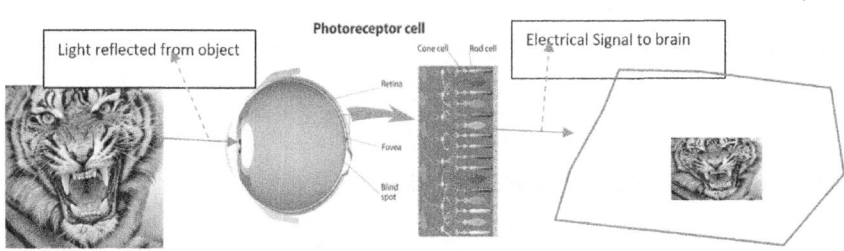

Figure 15: How the Human Brain Processes & Preceives Information

The light reflected from the tiger enters your pupil, which involuntarily dilates to gather more light and enhance your understanding of the surrounding information. Unconsciously, your eyes rapidly move within and around the image of the tiger, fixating on different points. These involuntary eye movements are called saccades and fixations. They occur due to the limited field of vision of our eyes, which spans about 1 degree on either side of the center of the image. The central region responsible for this field is known as the fovea, located on the backside of the eye.

The retina, located at the back of the eye, contains various types of cells, but the most significant ones are the photoreceptors—rods and cones. Rods, numbering around a billion, enable us to see in black and white and are active in dim light conditions. Cones, around 7 million in number, are responsible for detecting colors. In the given scenario, cones process the information collected during the rapid eye movements. The optic nerve continuously transmits this processed information as electrical signals to the brain. The brain then combines the information from these eye movements and automatically fills in any missing details. For instance, if the tiger is turning towards you, the brain calculates the speed and direction of the tiger. After processing this information, you become aware of the situation, and the flight response occurs involuntarily.

It is important to note that this dramatic example is not presented to add melodrama but rather to showcase the human mind's ability to fill in the missing pieces of the puzzle. This fascinating capacity of the brain to complete missing information has piqued the curiosity of psychology researchers throughout the last century.

Unveiling the Gestalt Principles

The Gestalt Principles are a collection of psychological laws that originated in the 1920s. They explain how humans tend to perceive objects by grouping similar elements, recognizing patterns, and simplifying complex images. These principles are similar to the way our minds processed the tiger scenario earlier. Designers leverage these principles to create engaging user experiences by employing perspective and following best design practices based on these principles.

By understanding how the human mind naturally perceives and organizes visual information, designers can leverage the Gestalt Principles to create designs that are visually appealing, intuitive, and easy to understand. These principles provide a framework for organizing elements, establishing a visual hierarchy, and guiding the viewer's attention. They help designers effectively communicate their intended message and evoke desired emotional responses from users.

The Gestalt Principles include concepts such as proximity, similarity, closure, continuation, and figure-ground relationship, among others. Each principle offers insights into how we perceive and interpret visual information. Designers apply these principles to create designs that make use of these inherent cognitive processes, leading to more impactful and visually cohesive compositions.

Law of Similarity

The law of similarity states that objects which follow a particular shape, size and color are grouped together as similar entities. Entities that share a common characteristic.

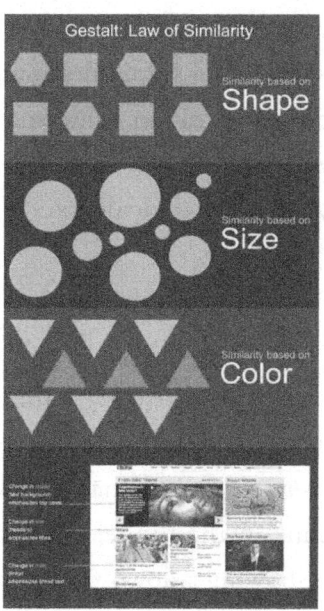

Figure 16: Laws Of Similarity

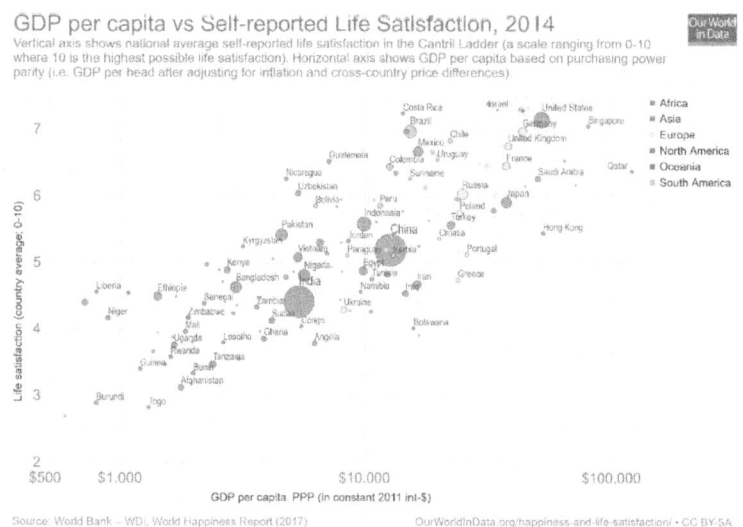

Figure 17: GDP Per Capita Vs Self-reported Life Satisfaction (Source: World Bank)

In the above example, the relationship between life satisfaction and GDP per capita is presented in a scatterplot. Since there are many data points, one for each country, additional information is presented in the form of colors and sizes. For example, the size of the bubble denotes the population density, and the color denotes the continent a country belongs to.

Law of Continuity

Our minds are adept at recognizing trends in time series data. Whether it is an upward or downward trend, our brains easily identify and interpret these patterns. Moreover, our minds have tendencies to assume that these trends will continue in the future. For instance, when presented with a time series chart showing a downward trend, our minds naturally expect the trend to persist indefinitely. Similarly, when confronted with an upward trend, we anticipate that it will continue to rise without end.

In the chart below, we can observe the trends in life satisfaction scores reported by individuals from various countries. By analyzing this chart, we can identify whether the life satisfaction scores exhibit upward or downward trends over time. Our minds intuitively grasp these patterns, allowing us to make sense of the data and anticipate the potential trajectory of future trends.

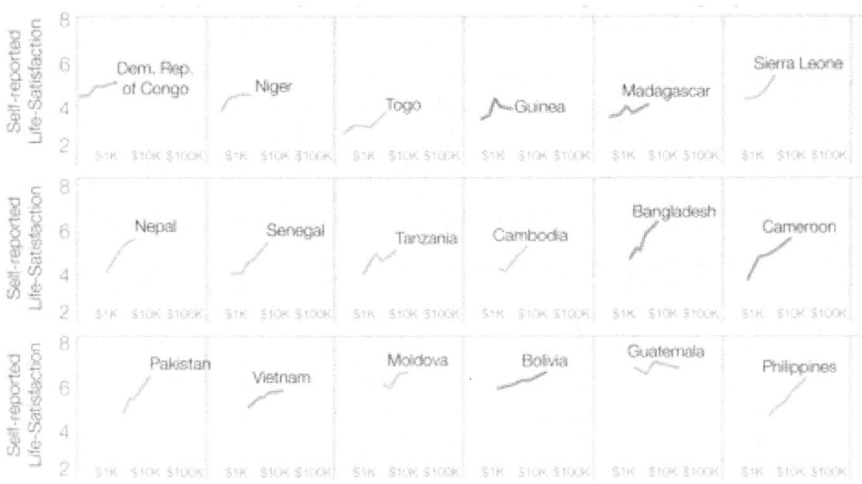

Figure 18: Trends In Life Satisfaction

By understanding the Law of Continuity, we can better comprehend how our minds perceive and interpret time series data, enabling us to derive valuable insights from charts and make informed decisions based on these trends. This unique chart falls into a special category known as "small multiples." By examining the chart, we can gather valuable insights about the trend in life satisfaction for different countries.

One notable observation is that the life satisfaction trend in Bangladesh shows a steep slope. This indicates that as the reported income level increases, individuals tend to report higher satisfaction scores at a faster rate. In other words, there is a significant disparity in the satisfaction scores between lower and higher income levels in Bangladesh. By analyzing this small multiples chart, we gain a deeper understanding of the relationship between reported income and life satisfaction and how it differs across various countries. These insights can inform policies, interventions, and decision-making processes aimed at enhancing overall well-being and quality of life.

Law of Proximity & Enclosure

The law of proximity states that we tend to see objects close to each other as a group and we also assume that they share the same characteristics. This kind of observation tends to be seen in charts like scatter plots, in which we can easily recognize a group of points together with their close.

The law of (en)closure tells us that the brain tends to complete forms which are basically incomplete. Case in point, the dashed line that we see as solid, axes lines that allow us to avoid frames around the chart are the connection that we make between the missing values. Our mind comes up with a smooth connection that fits the existing values in the best possible way.

Law of Connectivity

The law of connectivity emphasizes that our eyes are skilled at recognizing relationships between different elements by following lines, curves, or sequences of shapes. This principle applies to both positive and negative spaces in designs. Positive space refers to the area occupied by the main subject or image, while negative space is the surrounding area between its edges. When we look at a design, our eyes naturally follow lines that connect different elements. By applying this principle and utilizing colors effectively, designers can enhance the communication of information.

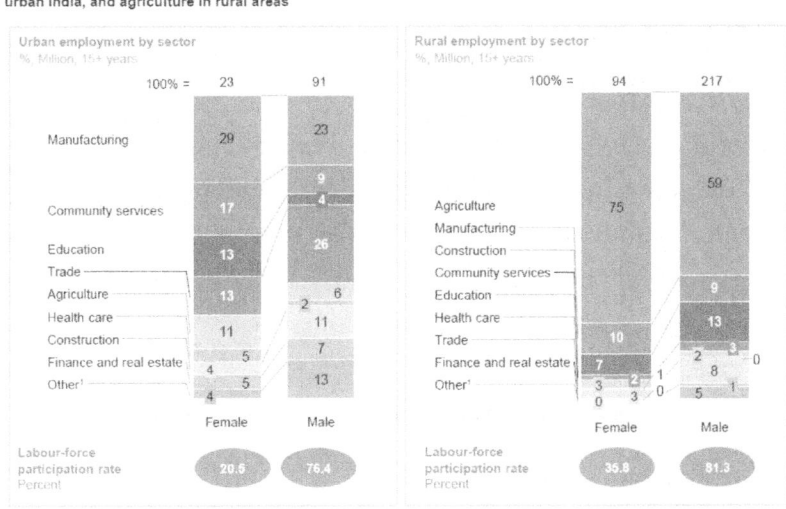

Figure 19: Urban Vs Rural Employment By Sector

The above figure shows that urban and rural employment data for different sectors is presented using a stacked bar chart format, which is familiar to many of us. However, what sets this chart apart is the use of small continuous lines that enable better comparison of various categories. For example, we can easily observe that the employment of males in community services is lower compared to females in urban sectors. Similarly, when comparing the education category between males and females in the same urban employment sector, the differences become more apparent. The chart also employs a thoughtful blend of warm and cool colors to convey these disparities. Warm colors represent categories with higher employment rates, while cool colors are used for relatively underemployed categories.

By applying the law of connectivity and leveraging colors effectively, this chart effectively communicates information. It allows viewers to make meaningful comparisons between different categories of urban and rural employment. The use of small continuous lines aids in visual comprehension, while the strategic use of warm and cool colors helps convey differences in employment levels.

By harnessing the power of the Gestalt Principles, designers can create designs that resonate with users, evoke desired emotions, and effectively communicate information. These principles serve as a valuable tool in the designer's toolkit, allowing them to craft visually compelling and user-friendly experiences across various mediums.

Building Blocks for Effective Data Visualization

Here are the key building blocks of data visualization:

Data Exploration

- Digging the data: Delving into the data to understand its structure, patterns, and insights.
- Measure & Dimensions: Identifying the quantitative measures and categorical dimensions within the data.

Semantic Attributes

- Specificity: Ensuring that the visual elements precisely represent the intended data values and attributes.
- Physical properties: Utilizing visual cues such as size, color, shape, and position to encode data attributes.
- Graphical integrity: Maintaining accuracy and integrity in representing the data without distorting or misleading information.
- Data-ink of a graph: Maximizing the use of visual elements that directly convey data, minimizing non-essential elements.

By combining data exploration and semantic attributes, data visualization practitioners can design effective visuals that provide meaningful insights and engage users in a user-centric manner.

Exploring Data: A Comprehensive Guide

Nathan Yau succinctly captures the essence of data visualization: "Data can be boring if you do not know what you are looking for or you do not know that there is something to look for in the first place." Visualizations go beyond numbers; they have the power to tell stories that convey truth and beauty. These stories can range from simple to complex, depending on the audience or the data scientist's decision on how to present them.

One of the finest visualizations ever created can be found on the website of GapMinder foundation website. This website was founded by the famous data scientist Hans Rosling and has accumulated a wealth of data on Human Development indicators. The website presents basically bubble charts which can be animated over time. This website is an example of the presentation of complex, large datasets. This visualization contains more than 400 years of human development data and allows one to compare the cross all the countries in the world. These visualizations allow one to connect with the charts.

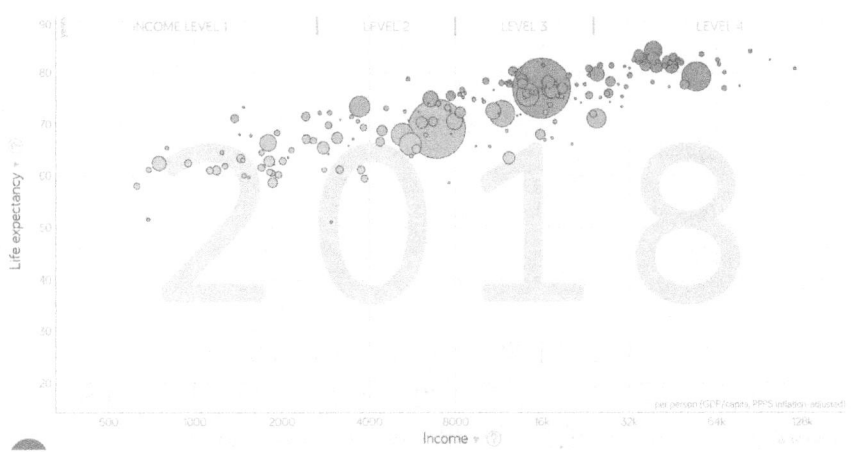

Figure 20: Life Expectancy Vs Income
(Source: gapminder.org)

The RiverFlow Diagram (AKA Sankey Diagram)

In contrast to the charts we discussed earlier, a river flow diagram visually represents the movement of people, money, or objects from one end to another. The diagram maintains the condition that the total on the left must be equal to the total on the right, although the segments connecting the flows can vary. This type of diagram works well for illustrating technology, furniture, and office supplies. The width of the river symbolizes the magnitude of the shift in a specific direction. River flow diagrams are particularly suitable for displaying financial data such as balance sheets, profit and loss statements, and cash flow statements. They can also be useful when comparing different categories in terms of percentages or when representing parts of a whole. In these cases, the Sankey diagram provides an alternative to the traditional pie chart.

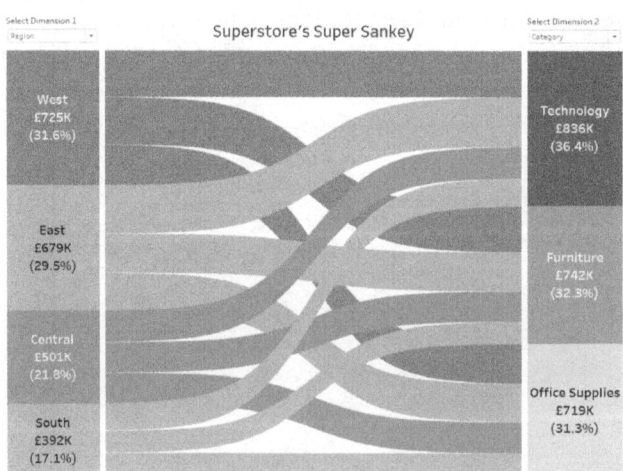

Figure 21: Superstore's Super Sankey
(Source: https://www.theinformationlab.co.uk/2018/03/09/build-sankey-diagram-tableau-without-data-prep-beforehand/)

Digging the Data

Data analysts are involved in identifying patterns and relationships within the data they analyze. In addition to this, they also play a crucial role in inspecting the data for any suspicious or anomalous numbers that may require further investigation. To uncover these patterns and relationships, analysts often compare and analyze data across different groups or categories, such as districts, states, countries, or firms. In large and complex datasets, these patterns may not be apparent at a granular level, so analysts need to aggregate the data at a higher level to reveal hidden patterns that are not readily visible in the raw data. Excel users may be familiar with the concept of "PivotTables," which allow for the slicing and dicing of data to gain insights and uncover meaningful patterns.

Measures and Dimensions

Measures are numerical values that quantify data in visualizations. They represent aggregated information such as sales totals or counts. Dimensions, on the other hand, categorize measures and provide structure to the data. They are used to slice and dice the data, such as by different categories or time periods.

Dimensions are qualitative and represent attributes like product models or time periods. Measures are quantitative and can be converted to dimensions by creating categories within them. For example, sales figures can be categorized as "above $300" and "below $300" to create a new dimension.

In some cases, new measures can be added to one-dimensional categorical data. Dimensions are considered independent variables, while measures are dependent variables. It is important to ensure that the data aggregation makes sense and is meaningful.

Many business intelligence tools have built-in features that automatically classify data into dimensions or measures, making it easier for data visualization practitioners and business users to analyze the data. These tools allow users to review and convert measures to dimensions and vice versa. However, it is worth noting that some tools may treat certain data, like latitude and longitude, as measures for the purpose of aggregation, even though they are dimensions.

Tableau, for example, automatically classifies data as dimensions or measures, as shown in the provided snapshot. While latitude and longitude are typically considered dimensions, Tableau treats them as measures to enable aggregation at different geographic levels, from country to state to city.

Figure 22: Screenshot From Tableau

Unraveling Semantic Attributes in Visualization

Semantic attributes in data visualization refer to the meaningfulness of visual representations. In the field of linguistic semantics, various attributes such as specificity, boundedness, animacy, gender, kinship, social status, physical properties, and function are studied. When it comes to data visualization, we focus on a subset of these attributes, particularly specificity and physical properties.

Specificity

Specificity in data visualization refers to the quality of visual entities uniquely belonging to specific subjects or categories. It involves using visual representations that distinctively convey meaning and differentiate between different aspects of the data. By employing specific visuals tailored to the characteristics of the data, we can enhance understanding and effectively communicate information.

For example, in a dashboard, geographic heatmaps can be utilized to represent the average cost per state. This choice of visualization allows for clear differentiation between states and enables easy comparison of cost variations across different regions. Similarly, when visualizing demand stages, a funnel chart can provide a specific representation that highlights the progression and conversion rates at each stage. The distinct shape of the funnel chart aids in conveying the specific meaning of the different stages in a visually impactful manner.

By leveraging specificity in data visualization, we can create visuals that are meaningful and facilitate better comprehension of the data. Selecting appropriate visual representations that uniquely relate to the subjects being portrayed enhances the overall clarity and effectiveness of the visualization.

Figure 23: Sample Dashboard - Specificity

Using visuals that convey specific meaning is essential for effective data visualization. While there are various options for selecting visuals, it is important to choose the most appropriate one that aligns with the information being represented. For example, a bar chart can be used as an alternative to a geographic heatmap, but it may not be as suitable for conveying the intended message accurately.

Physical Properties

Physical properties with reference to visualization include the following:

- Shape
- Size
- Color
- Graphical symbols
- Orientation
- Composition
- Animated vs Static

Shape

Shape encompasses both geometric and non-geometric figures. Geometric figures, such as squares, triangles, circles, cylinders, and rectangles, have regular contours and defined edges. On the other hand, non-geometric figures have irregular contours or lack proper edges. Both geometric and non-geometric shapes carry obvious or subtle meanings and can convey different messages to viewers when the same information is represented in different shapes. Therefore, selecting the right shape for a visual improves its specificity.

For example, a circle, being a closed shape with no defined beginning or end, is recommended for representing information that is closed and does not require exploration. Conversely, for information with future uncertainty, a line or an arrow is suggested. Utilizing different shapes to represent the same information allows for conveying nuanced aspects and enhances the clarity and effectiveness of the visual representation.

Size

Size, in an abstract manner, denotes the importance of the visual. The larger the visual, the more important it is, and objects of the same size share similar weightage. Furthermore, arranging similarly shaped objects from left to right denotes growth in a certain culture. The image below serves as an example of organizing similar images from left to right in ascending order, signifying growth.

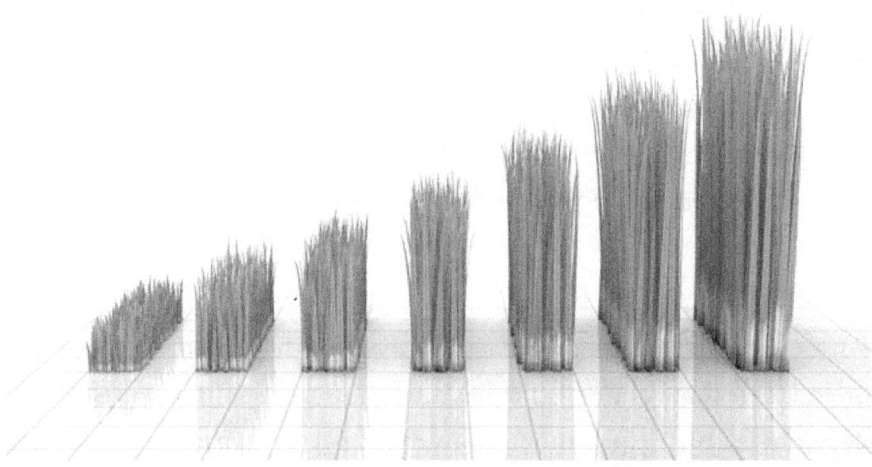

Figure 24: Column Chart With Size

Kindly note that Arabic cultures follow right to left direction to symbolize growth and hence, cultural and regional context must be applied while working on the physical properties of the visual.

Below is a world map based on projected gross domestic product (GDP) as of 2017. Political boundaries of the maps are resized to show the GDP; hence, Russia looks very small when compared with India, and the entire countries in the African continents are looking small. Although it is not recommended to redraw the world map, this is an interesting example to explain the importance of size.

Understanding Visual Perception

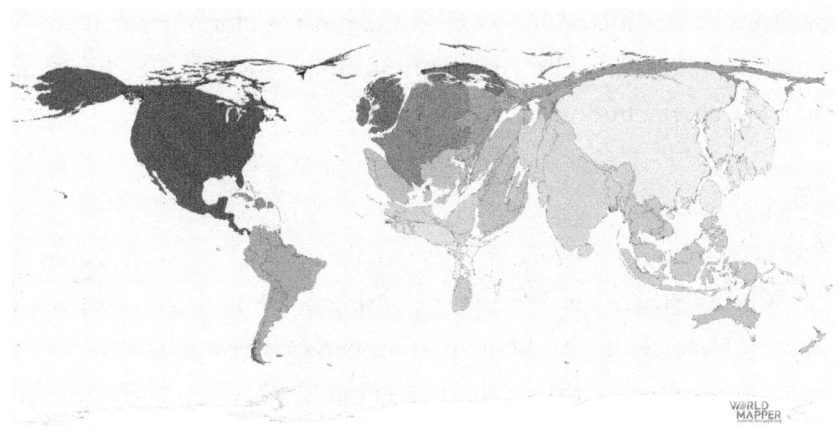

Figure 25: World GDP Map
(Source: https://worldmapper.org/)

The below image is an example of how size is used to summarize foreign currency reserves in different countries. The size of the countries is modified according to the relative size of foreign currency reserves; hence, Russia—being the largest country in terms of area—looks very small.

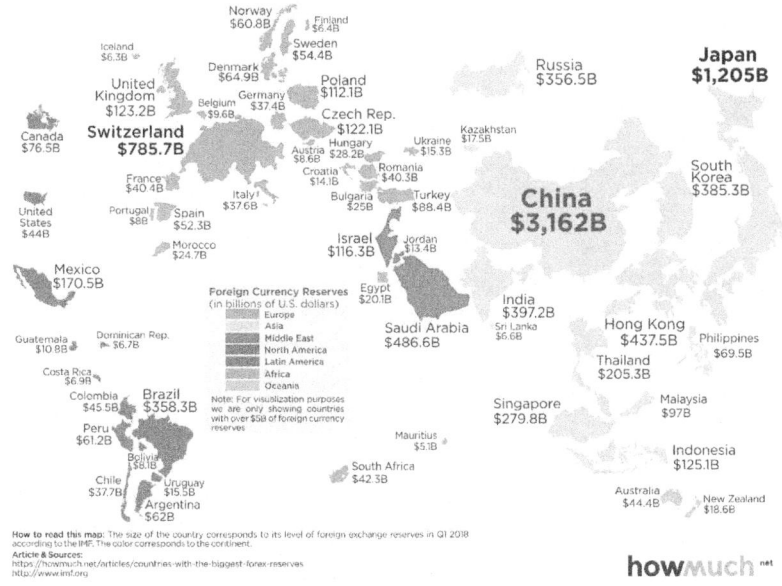

Figure 26: Foreign Currency World Map
(Source: howmuch.net)

Numerous charts incorporate size as the most important parameter for comparing values and displaying proportions, such as pie charts, area charts, bar charts, bubble charts, box plots, etc.

Color

Color plays a significant role in data visualization, along with shapes and sizes. While aesthetics is one aspect of using color, it also serves practical purposes. Color helps in differentiating between visuals and provides a scale of importance within a chart or graph. A heatmap is a compelling example that showcases how color acts as a measure to distinguish severity levels from low to high.

By incorporating appropriate color schemes and gradients, data visualizations can effectively convey information and highlight patterns or trends. Color adds depth and visual hierarchy, enhancing the overall understanding and impact of the visual representation. Below is an example of a heatmap with color helping to distinguish high and low CO_2 emissions per capita.

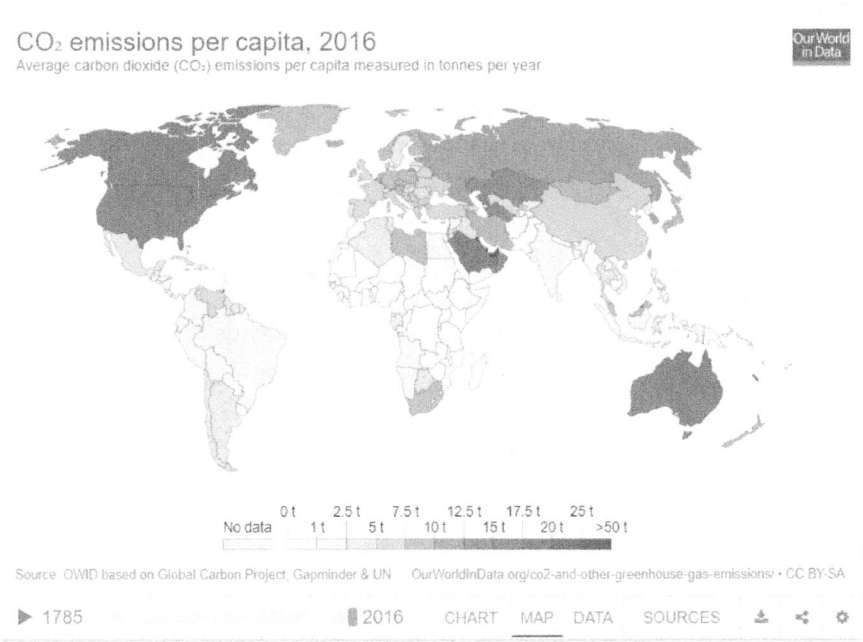

Figure 27: CO2 Emissions Per Capita

Below is an example of how colors are used to distinguish different clusters in a scatter plot.

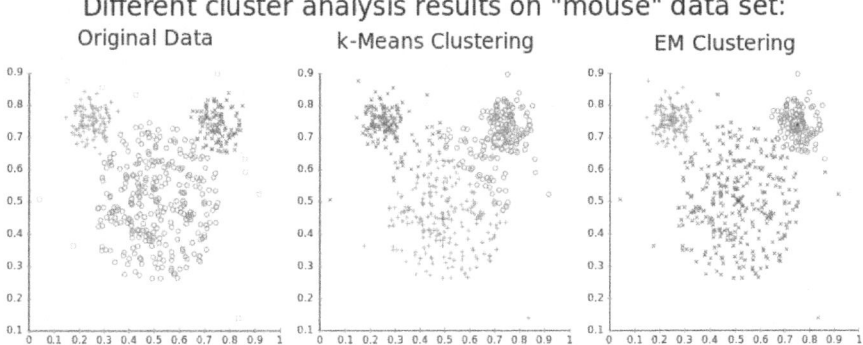

Figure 28: Cluster Analysis

There are generally understood color codes, such as red for alarms and green for indicating things in place. However, when designing visuals, it is important to consider the cultural context and sensitivity associated with colors. For instance, in China, red symbolizes luck and fertility, whereas in Nigeria, it represents violence and sacrifice.

Graphical Symbols

The saying "A picture is worth a thousand words" emphasizes the effectiveness of symbols and images in communication. Graphical symbols play a crucial role in data visualization and conveying messages visually. They combine shape, size, and color to represent objects, ideas, or information, and their meaning is generally understood across language barriers. To enhance their effectiveness, graphical symbols are often accompanied by notes and titles. They have a personal appeal and can be tied to physical experiences, as seen in the example of an ATM using a symbol to encourage users to go paperless.

In the realm of social media and platforms, new emoticons, smileys, and stickers have emerged as powerful means of communication. These graphical symbols have attracted the attention of analytics professionals who extract intelligence, such as topic mining and sentiment analysis, from these symbols. They convey meaning with personal appeal and are particularly useful when quick decisions or information transfer is necessary. Skype's emoticons serve as an example, allowing users to express emotions through symbols that can be further analyzed through text-mining techniques.

Figure 29: Skype Emoticons

Below is a sample from Twitter. The platform, along with Facebook, provides an advanced scope for analytics for businesses both before and after the launch of a product.

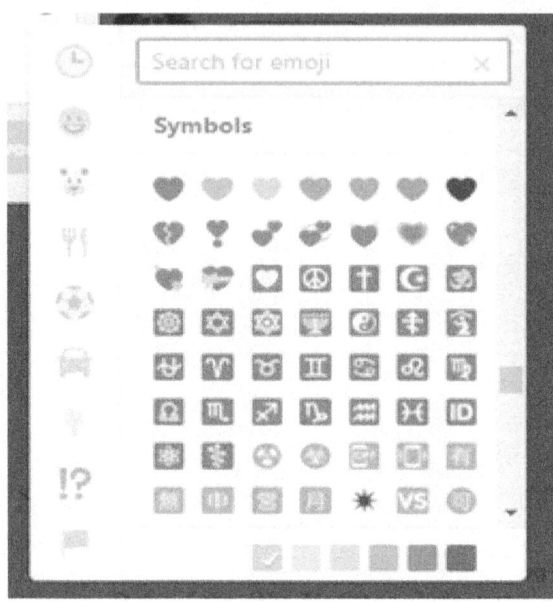

Figure 30: Twitter Emoji

It is important for data scientists and data visualization practitioners to take note of the various graphical symbols that exist and use them effectively in presentations, dashboards, and KPIs. Below is an example of a dashboard created for call center operations (image credit: Klipfolio) where symbols are used to represent metrics such as the number of agents logged in, the number of agents ready, calls exceeding 5 minutes, etc. The graphical symbols used here capture the viewer's attention and facilitate a quicker understanding of the presented information.

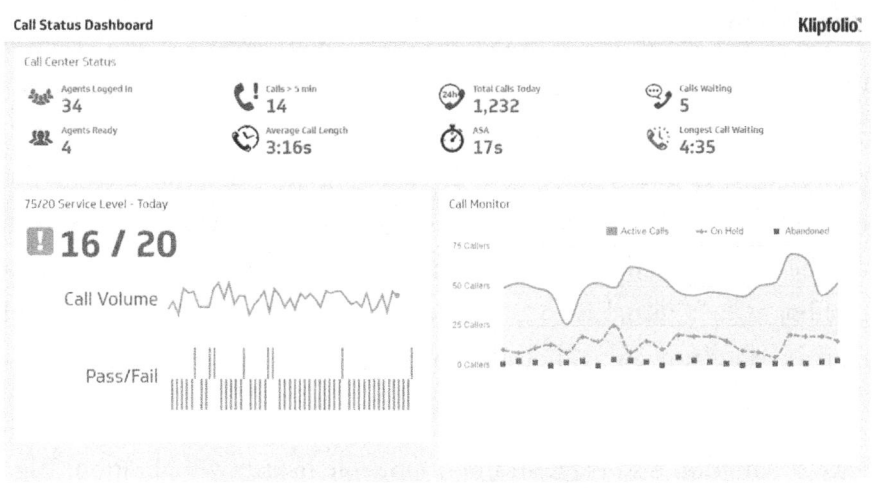

Figure 31: Dashboard Sample Klipfolio

Below is a sample social media dashboard (image credit: Hootsuite) where information, demographic information and various social media platforms are represented along with symbols.

Figure 32: Dashboard Sample Hootsuite

Orientation

Orientation refers to the way visuals are displayed in a dashboard, presentation, or tool. It is the act of positioning a KPI or visual relative to other KPIs and visuals and determining the directionality of the information in the visuals. To orient a map means to align the directions on the map with the directions on the ground. Similarly, to orient a dashboard or a visual is to correctly position and align the charts and metrics that provide a holistic and accurate view of the presented information.

Page orientation also plays an important role in data visualization. Page orientation refers to how a frame is positioned for normal viewing, such as portrait or landscape. Nowadays, the concept of aspect ratio is also used instead of page orientation.

Static Vs Animated

Static visuals are commonly used to represent business data, and they are effective in understanding data up to four dimensions. A bubble chart is an example of a static visual that can accommodate up to four dimensions. It is a variation of a scatter chart where data points are replaced with bubbles, and size and color are used to represent additional dimensions of the data.

The image below (image source: Microsoft Power BI) displays data with four dimensions. The x-axis represents sales per square foot, the y-axis represents total sales variance %, the size of the bubble represents the sales value, and the color represents different districts.

Understanding Visual Perception

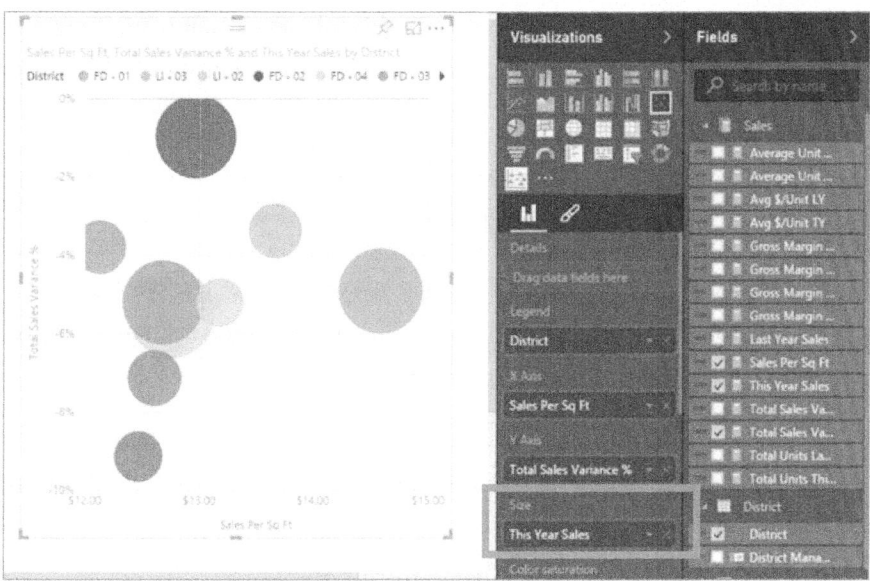

Figure 33: Bubble Chart

Animated visuals are also becoming famous, where additional dimensions can be added, but as of date, static visuals are generally used in business data visualization.

Graphical Integrity

Visual representations of data must be truthful and accurate to ensure the integrity of the information being presented. Edward Tufte, in his book "The Visual Display of Quantitative Information," provides a series of examples that highlight how data can be distorted in visualizations, leading to incorrect interpretations. By manipulating various aspects of a visualization, such as scaling, labeling, or choosing inappropriate chart types, the true representation of the data can be compromised. Tufte emphasizes the importance of avoiding these distortions and encourages data practitioners to strive for clarity and honesty in their visualizations.

By adhering to principles of honesty and accuracy in data visualization, as demonstrated in Tufte's book, we can ensure that the insights derived from the visuals are reliable and meaningful for decision-making and analysis. According to Tufte, we can calculate a Lie factor as:

$$\text{Lie Factor} = \frac{\text{Size of the Effect in the graphic}}{\text{Size of the Effect on the Data}}$$

If the Lie Factor is greater than 1, the graph overstates the effect. Ideally, each graph should have a lie factor of 1. Lie factors greater than 1.05 and less than 0.95 distort the data substantially.

Tufte offers guidelines for creating accurate and reliable visual representations of data. These principles can help ensure that visuals effectively communicate information without distorting its meaning. Here are some key principles to keep in mind:

- Use consistent scales.
- Use proportional labeling.
- Provide clear labeling and highlight important points.
- Focus on data variation, not design.
- Standardize monetary units and consider inflation.
- Do not exceed data dimensions.
- Present data in context.

Following these principles ensures truthful and informative visual representations.

Data-Ink of a Graph

Tufte emphasizes the importance of data-ink, which refers to the ink on a graph that represents actual data. He encourages maximizing the data-ink ratio by minimizing non-essential elements. This includes erasing unnecessary information and avoiding redundancy. Tufte's principles guide us to prioritize showing the data and making efficient use of ink in visualizations. Understanding concepts like the lie factor and data ink can serve as valuable foundations for effective data visualization.

Choosing the Right Visual: Making Informed Decisions

When choosing a visual for data visualization, it is important to consider the business requirements, explore the data, and plan accordingly. The available data sets the opportunities and limitations for visual selection, while the business requirements guide us in creating visuals that make an impact on the audience. During the planning phase, it is helpful to ask the following questions:

- What is the business need?
- Who will be using the visuals?
- Who will provide the data for the visuals?
- How often will the data be available?
- How should missing data be handled?
- How should late-arriving data be managed?
- What actions do we expect users to take based on the visuals?
- What devices will the visuals be viewed on?
- How frequently should the visuals be updated (real-time requirement)?
- Should we incorporate machine learning and AI features into the visuals?
- Will users need to print the visuals?
- Will users integrate the visuals into third-party tools and reports?

The planning phase of a project is agile and can occur at various stages, including requirement gathering, data exploration, logic definition, implementation, user acceptance testing, and post go-live. Answering the questions mentioned above during this phase helps drive the design and prevents unnecessary rework. A well-designed dashboard and structured KPI viewers should tell a coherent story that aligns with the business objectives. The insights shared in the visuals should be relevant to the business needs and provide actionable information. While the data might uncover fascinating insights, it is crucial to ensure that these insights contribute to the overall story and are specific to the requirements.

For instance, let us consider the case of an internal audit function in a telecom operator. Their business requirement is to ensure that all customer calls are charged according to the rating plan. One of their KPIs is to reconcile the number of calls and minutes of usage between the operations support system and the billing or business support system. The visual representation should highlight any discrepancies at a summary level and allow users to drill down for further investigation. It is important to avoid including unrelated dramatic insights in a dashboard and KPI container, as they are not aligned with the internal audit focus. However, such insights can be packaged separately and provided to marketing as part of a cross-sales initiative. The image below, sourced from Gamma Analytics, illustrates a visual showing the reconciliation between the telecom operations support system and the business support system. The chart displays daily variance in call count and minutes of usage using bars, while the line represents the percentage variance. A table below the chart provides the same information and allows users to drill down to a more detailed level.

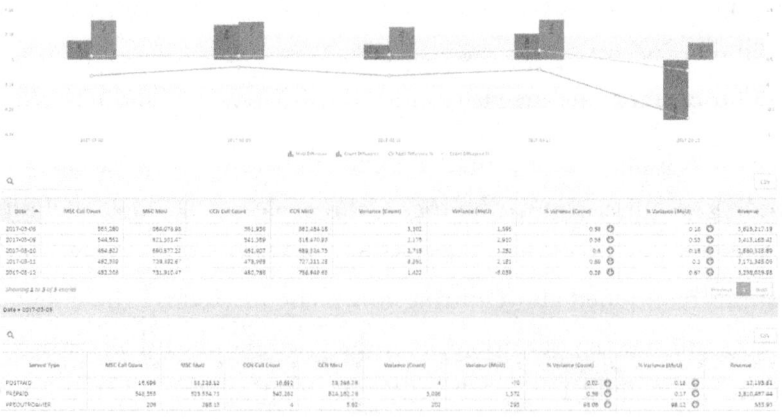

Figure 34: Telecom Data Reconciliation KPI

Captivating Your Audience: Visualization with Audience in Mind

When creating visualizations, it is crucial to prioritize the audience's needs and use language that resonates with them. Using unfamiliar terminology or complex jargon, even if the insights are relevant, will only lead to disinterest from the audience. Instead, we should choose terminology that the audience is familiar with, such as trends in sales across different rate plans or customer segments. Understanding the level of detail required by the audience and catering the information accordingly is also important. It is worth noting that senior management and C-level executives prefer simpler visuals, while technical teams and analysts may appreciate more complex ones.

Role-based login plays a significant role in providing tailored visual experiences. It allows us to present different types of visuals or different sets of information to different audiences. One size does not fit all, and a single design may not please everyone. Therefore, it is essential to offer diverse KPIs, charts, dashboards, and visuals to cater to the specific needs of each audience group. During the planning stage, involving all user groups and understanding their requirements will guide the design process, ensuring that the visuals effectively capture the audience's attention and convey meaningful stories.

To enhance user experience, it is important to minimize clutter by removing irrelevant elements from reports. The physical properties of the visuals should facilitate easy navigation and enable users to grasp information at a glance. Clarity and cohesiveness are key to delivering the intended message. Applying Gestalt principles, leveraging the building blocks of data visualization, and considering the concepts of choosing effective visualizations all contribute to creating visuals that are focused on capturing and maintaining audience attention.

Exercises

Refer to the URL: https://www.mckinsey.com/featured-insights/2023-year-in-review/2023-the-year-in-charts#/ for the following questions.

1. Grouping in Office Space Conversion Impact:
   How does the Gestalt principle of grouping allow us to compare and contrast the impact of office space conversion across different cities? Discuss how proximity and similarity in this graph aid in the perception of data clusters.

2. Figure-Ground in Real Estate Adaptation Strategies:
   Analyze the application of the figure-ground principle in this graph. How does this principle help in distinguishing the main focus from the background information?

3. Similarity and Continuity in Housing Stock Increase Trends:
   Discuss how the principles of similarity and continuity guide the viewer's understanding of the trend across different cities. How does the visual treatment of data points affect the perception of this trend?

4. Closure in Understanding Complex Real Estate Data:
   Examine how the principle of closure allows viewers to comprehend complex real estate data. Can you identify areas where the graph leverages this principle to simplify data interpretation?

5. Symmetry and Order in Global Real Estate Trends:
   How do the principles of symmetry and order help in making sense of global real estate trends? Analyze the arrangement and presentation of data in relation to these Gestalt principles.

CHAPTER 3

HARNESSING THE POWER OF VISUALIZATION IN ANALYTICS

Exploratory Analysis: Unveiling Insights through Visualization

There is a famous parable in India called "The Elephant and the Five Blind Men"; the parable has various Indian versions, but the general story goes like this:

A group of blind men learned that a peculiar animal, known as an elephant, had arrived in their town, but they had no idea about its shape and form. Out of curiosity, they decided to touch and explore it, using their sense of touch. Each blind man touched a different part of the elephant.

The one who touched the trunk exclaimed, "This being is like a thick snake." Another blind man who touched the ear described it as a kind of fan. The blind man who touched the leg compared the elephant to a pillar or a tree trunk. The one who touched the side declared it to be a wall, while the blind man who felt the tail described it as a rope. Finally, the blind man who touched the tusk described it as something hard, smooth, and sharp like a spear. This parable emphasizes the idea that different perspectives can lead to varying interpretations of the same object or situation.

In a similar context, the process of exploratory analysis can be compared to this parable. Much like the blind men trying to understand the elephant by touching different parts, exploratory data analysis involves exploring the dataset using various tools and techniques. While there is plenty of content available on the internet that emphasizes the use of plots and graphs for exploratory data analysis, many of them overlook the significance of the process itself. In this chapter, we outline the broad steps involved in creating an exploratory analysis for a given dataset.

To better understand the process of exploratory data analysis, let us draw a parallel with the field of photography. Interestingly, a good data scientist needs to think like a photographer! We all appreciate photographs, and with the advancements in smartphone technology, capturing decent photos has become easier than ever before. However, even with these technological advancements, amateur photographers, like most of us, still struggle to match the quality of professional photographs taken by experts. Why is that?

The reason lies in the extensive trial-and-error process that professional photographers undertake. Before a professional photograph gets published in a leading journal, magazine, or competition, a series of meticulous steps are followed. Expert photographers take numerous photos of a scene, experimenting with different combinations of aperture, shutter speed, and ISO settings. Even entry-level DSLRs offer a wide range of options in these settings, allowing photographers to capture different moods and effects. The photographer relies on their judgment and experience to select a few photos that meet their criteria, discarding the rest. As a result, many rejected photos remain unseen by the end viewer. This selection process can be likened to exploratory data analysis in data science, where the data scientist conducts extensive background work and presents only a handful of carefully chosen graphs and visualizations in the final report.

Once the photographs are narrowed down, professional photographers use software like Adobe Photoshop to fine-tune and enhance the selected images. The initial work of capturing the photos using the camera is just the beginning; the bulk of the work lies in post-processing and editing the shortlisted photographs in professional software to achieve the desired outcome. Similarly, in the field of exploratory data analysis, obtaining a dataset is just the starting point. A significant amount of refining and fine-tuning is required to meet the data scientist's requirements and objectives.

Broadly, the steps involved in exploratory data analysis can be summarized as follows:

- Define the problem statement and set a SMART goal.
- Develop relevant hypotheses related to the stated problem.
- Prepare, transform, enrich, and summarize the data.
- Test the hypotheses using visualization techniques.
- Validate the findings using statistical tests and consider building advanced machine learning models.

By following these steps, data scientists can gain valuable insights from the data and make informed decisions.

Visualizations for Effective Exploratory Analysis
Charts

Charts are widely recognized as graphical representations of data, serving as valuable tools for exploring and presenting aggregated information.

While there is a vast array of chart types available, some of the fundamental ones commonly used in data visualization include:

- Column chart: Displays data as vertical columns, making it easy to compare values across different categories or time periods.
- Bar chart: Similar to the column chart, but with horizontal bars, allowing for quick comparisons.
- Stacked bar chart: Shows multiple sets of data as stacked bars, revealing both the individual and cumulative values.
- Pie chart: Represents data as slices of a pie, highlighting the proportion of each category within a whole.
- Scatter chart: Visualizes the relationship between two variables through individual data points plotted on a Cartesian coordinate system.
- Geo chart: Displays data on a geographic map, enabling analysis based on geographical regions.
- Area chart: Depicts the cumulative total of data over time or across categories, emphasizing the magnitude of change.
- Combo chart: Combines multiple chart types, such as columns and lines, in a single visualization to present diverse datasets.
- Line chart: Connects data points with lines, allowing for the depiction of trends and patterns over time.
- Bubble chart: Represents data points as bubbles with varying sizes, incorporating a third variable to illustrate additional information.
- Donut chart: Similar to a pie chart but with a hollow center, making it suitable for displaying multiple data series.
- Hierarchical Charts: Visualize a hierarchy to identify patterns in thematic structures or view demographics of cases and content. Size conveys meaning, while color provides additional information.
- Organization chart: Represents hierarchical relationships within an organization or structure, showcasing reporting lines and roles.
- Treemap: Displays hierarchical data as nested rectangles, with sizes representing the values of the data elements.

- Boxplot: Presents statistical information, such as median, quartiles, and outliers, to showcase the distribution of data.

These chart types can be found in various business intelligence (BI) tools like Power BI and Tableau, as well as developer toolboxes provided by platforms such as FusionCharts, Google Charts, Highcharts, and more. Using these tools, data analysts and scientists can leverage the power of visualization to effectively communicate insights and patterns hidden within complex datasets.

Below is an example of a boxplot with the x-axis showing different categories of rate plans in a digital service provider and the y-axis showing the revenue.

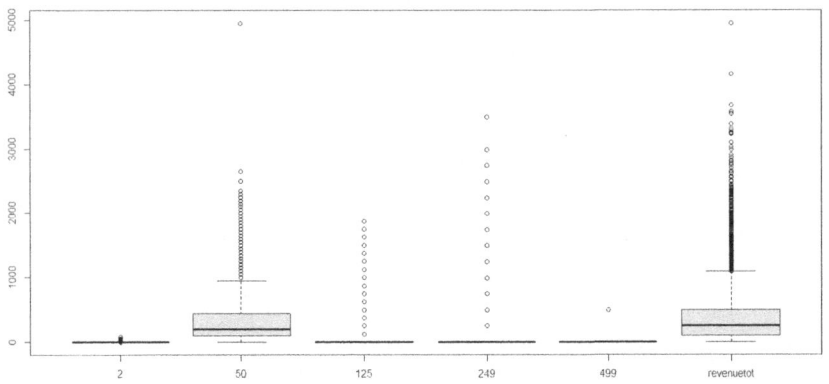

Figure 35: Box Plot - Rate Plan

Below is an example of a combo chart where the amount spent against different invoice categories is visualized using a bar chart supported by a line chart to show the percentage for ease of reference.

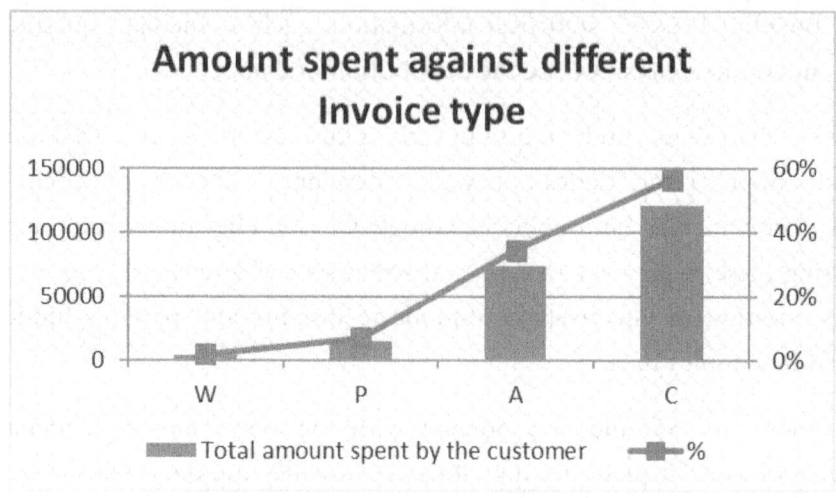

Figure 36: Combo Chart - Amount Spent

Below is another example of a combo chart.

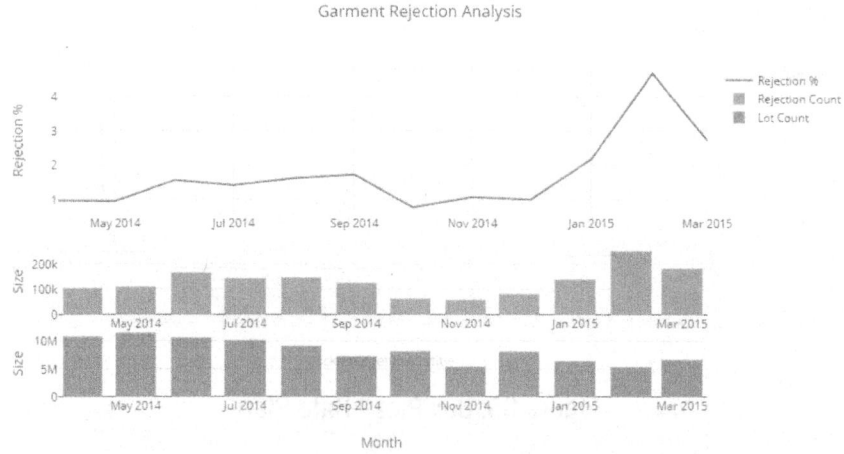

Figure 37: Combo Chart - Garment Rejection Analysis

Word cloud

Word Clouds are powerful visualizations for textual data analysis. They provide a visually appealing representation of words found within a dataset, highlighting the most frequently occurring terms in relation to other commonly used words. By employing variations in color and font size, Word Clouds visually convey the frequency of each word in the text data. This technique finds great utility in social media analysis, allowing researchers to gain insights into popular topics, trends, or themes.

Moreover, Word Clouds can be enhanced by incorporating additional dimensions of analysis. For instance, sentiment analysis can be integrated to associate positive, negative, or neutral sentiments with specific words, providing a deeper understanding of the emotional context within the text. Furthermore, segments or categories can be incorporated into the Word Clouds, allowing for the visualization of word frequencies based on different groups or subsets within the data.

Overall, Word Clouds offer a captivating and intuitive way to explore textual data, enabling researchers to quickly identify key terms and patterns. By leveraging various techniques such as sentiment analysis and segmentation, Word Clouds can provide even more valuable insights for data analysis and decision-making.

Below is an example of a word cloud with sentiment analysis included in the visual:

Figure 38: Word Cloud - Sentiment Analysis

Other Visual Techniques

- Word Trees: Display a keyword with related context branching out based on frequency. The size of the branches indicates the number of times a particular sentence occurs, helping identify recurring themes or phrases.
- Concept Maps: Map out connections to present ideas, interpretations, or theories. These visualizations consist of shapes and connectors that articulate links such as cause and effect, requirements, or contributions.
- Mind Maps: A brainstorming tool that starts with a central topic or main idea. They can be used to organize groups of related concepts into themes.

- Explore Diagrams: Focus on a single item and show all the other items connected to it. Users can navigate through different connections between items.
- Comparison Diagrams: Show similarities and differences between two items. They can be used to compare content, themes, or cases.
- Project Maps: Visually explore and present different items and connections within a research project. They help identify emerging patterns, theories, and explanations.
- Sociograms: Graphic representations of social links that a person has. They plot the structure of interpersonal relations in a group and assist in social network analysis.
- Geovisualizations: Tools and techniques for analyzing geospatial data through interactive visualization. They provide a deeper understanding of location groupings and are particularly useful with demographic information.

These visualization techniques enhance data analysis and communication by providing intuitive and visually engaging representations of complex information.

Driving Success with SMART Goals in Data Visualization

The concept of SMART goals has its roots in organizational management. Dr. Edwin Locke introduced goal setting in the 1960s, and George T. Doran coined the term SMART in the 1980s. SMART goals are quantifiable objectives that lead to superior performance when systematically set and followed up on.

SMART goals are applicable in the field of data science, where projects can be well-suited for goal setting and measurable improvements. However, many goals set in data science projects are vague and lack measurability. This can confuse teams and result in wasted efforts. The process of setting SMART goals helps progress from vague to clear objectives.

The process involves crafting goals that are Specific, Measurable, Attainable, Relevant, and Time-bound (SMART). Each letter in the acronym represents a milestone in goal setting:

- Specific: Clearly define what the goal is, how it will be implemented, why it is important, and who is responsible. For example, increasing the number of term depositors by 20% through direct marketing phone calls made by call center executives.
- Measurable: Ensure the goal is quantifiable. Specify measurable criteria, such as the number of phone calls. For example, using 500 phone calls as a measure of direct marketing efforts.
- Attainable: Assess available resources, required skills, and knowledge needed to achieve the goal. Determine if there are enough call center executives and if the necessary skills and knowledge are in place.
- Relevant: Justify the relevance of the goal based on the organization's objectives and market studies. Consider factors such as customer demand and growth potential.
- Time-bound: Set a clear deadline for achieving the goal. Avoid delays or procrastination. For example, aiming to achieve the goal within two months.

By following the SMART goal-setting process, data science projects can begin with a well-defined objective. This approach increases clarity, measurability, and the likelihood of success.

Hypotheses and SMART Goals

Hypothesis testing is a crucial concept in inferential statistics. It can be a complex idea to grasp, but there are simplified explanations available. One such resource is a helpful introduction to Carleton's SERC website. The example presented in that article involves a student studying animal behavior in a biology class. The student is assigned research on mallard ducks and their attraction to the color green. The hypothesis the student frames is whether female ducks are also attracted to the green color in food, such as bread.

Hypothesis testing involves data collection and analysis, which aligns with the principles of exploratory data analysis. To demonstrate the process of hypothesis development, we will work with the Bigmart dataset in the following section. This dataset serves as a suitable starting point for exploring and understanding these concepts.

Introduction to the BigMart Dataset: Exploring Sales and Predictive Modeling

The BigMart dataset provides valuable insights into the sales of 1559 products across ten outlets located in different cities in 2013. Along with sales data, the dataset also includes various attributes associated with each product and store. The primary objective is to develop a predictive model that can accurately estimate the sales of individual products at specific outlets. By analyzing this data, BigMart aims to identify the key factors that influence sales performance, both at the product and outlet levels. Detailed information about the dataset can be found on the Analytics Vidya website. The dataset presents numerous opportunities for exploration and analysis.

To approach this data science project systematically, we will begin by formulating a SMART goal that guides our exploration and analysis:

SMART Goal for the Dataset

"Within a two-month timeframe, increase sales by 10% at ten outlets of a Tier 3 grocery store, utilizing relevant product and outlet characteristics such as item fat content, item visibility, outlet location, outlet size, and more."

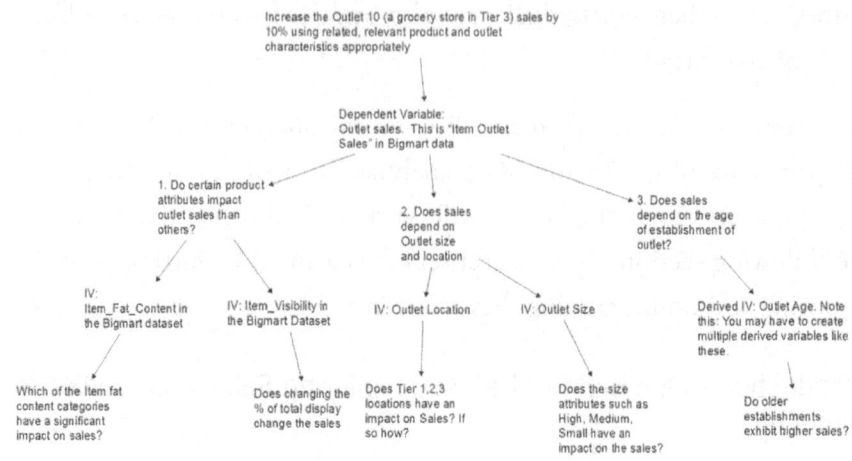

Figure 39: SMART Goal

Unleashing the Potential of Visualizing Categorical Data
Understanding Categorical Data: Unveiling Groups and Categories

Categorical data plays a crucial role in data analysis, representing discrete variables that can be divided into distinct groups. It encompasses a wide range of information, including qualitative observations, social media conversations, published research findings, and even automated data from computer systems, robots, and sensors. Additionally, categorical data can be derived from converting continuous data into distinct categories.

Categorical variables can take different forms, such as binary variables or polytomous variables. In some cases, polytomous variables are transformed into binary variables for analysis and effective visualization. Moreover, categorical variables can be further classified as nominal or ordinal. Nominal variables lack any intrinsic ordering among their categories, although each category can be represented by a number or label. For instance, consider the categorical variable "color," which has three categories: Blue (represented by 1), Yellow (represented by 2), and Green (represented by 3). It is important to note that these categories have no inherent order, meaning we must analyze the data without assigning additional weight to any particular category.

To provide a visual example, the table below illustrates a sample representation of nominal data using a dictionary-like format:

Table 2: Reference Table for Color

Color	Dictionary_Value
Blue	1
Yellow	2
Green	3

Table 3: Data Dictionary

Car Manufacturer	Color
Honda	2
Hyundai	1
Toyota	3
Hyundai	3
Toyota	2
Honda	2
Hyundai	1
Toyota	2
Hyundai	3
Toyota	1
Toyota	3
Hyundai	1
Toyota	1
Honda	1
Hyundai	1
Toyota	2

Table 4: Summary Output Before Transformation

Count of cars against different colors

Car	1	2	3	Total
Honda	1	2	0	3
Hyundai	4	0	2	6
Toyota	2	3	2	7
Total	7	5	4	**16**

Summary Output (transformed): Count of cars against different colors with transformation

Please note that the header has been transformed from 1,2 and 3 to Blue, Yellow and green, respectively.

Table 5: Summary Output Transformed

Car	Blue	Yellow	Green	Total
Honda	1	2	0	3
Hyundai	4	0	2	6
Toyota	2	3	2	7
Total	7	5	4	**16**

As you can see from the above example, we replaced the heading of the summary output (transformed) with Blue, Yellow and Green from 1, 2 and 3 in the Summary Output (before transformation).

If we fail to acknowledge that the dictionary value for the colors is not nominal, we may end up giving weights to the color and may perform a sum of dictionary values, in which case the summary table will look as below:

Table 6: Erroneous

Car	Blue	Yellow	Green	Total
Honda	1	4		5
Hyundai	4		6	10
Toyota	2	6	6	14
Total	7	10	12	29

Note that the total is 29 against the correct value of 16.

An ordinal variable has a clear ordering. For example, the height of basketball players is a variable with three orderly categories (low, medium and high).

Analysis and visualization of categorical data begin with the creation of summary tables. Summarizing, in general, involved counting records per category, for example, the count of male employees and female employees in the company. Basic representation is to quantify value into a category. Further summarizing operations involved sum, average, weighted average, variance, range, percentage, etc.

The above explanation is a simple concept, but we have come across experts in BI delivering dashboards and KPIs with wrong summarization, partially due to the tasks assigned to the team without specific instructions about these.

Visualizing Categorical Time Series Data

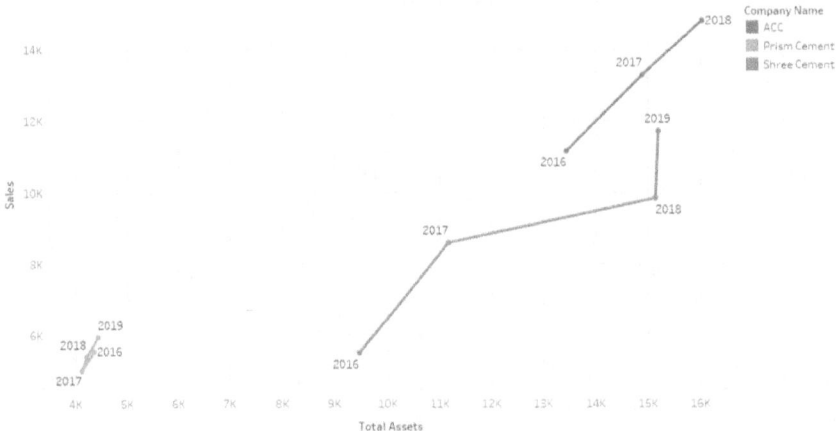

Figure 40: Connected Scatter Plot

The above chart represents a connected scatter plot, which combines the features of a scatter plot and a time series plot. Let us analyze the insights provided by the chart:

a. Prism Cement: Across all four years, Prism Cement shows lower asset values and lower sales compared to the other two companies. This indicates that Prism Cement has been less successful in terms of asset growth and generating sales.

b. Shree Cement: The progress of Shree Cement stands out prominently. There is a significant difference in both assets and sales when comparing the figures from 2016 to 2019. The company has consistently added assets every year until 2018, demonstrating a remarkable growth trajectory.

c. In 2019, Shree Cement effectively utilized its existing asset base to increase sales. This indicates that the company leveraged its resources efficiently to drive sales growth.

d. ACC: ACC has demonstrated consistent performance throughout the analyzed period. The company has maintained a relatively stable position in terms of assets and sales.

Overall, the connected scatter plot provides valuable insights into the performance and trends of Prism Cement, Shree Cement, and ACC. It highlights differences in asset values and sales over time, showcasing the strengths and areas for improvement for each company.

Visualizing Relationships Between Multiple Variables

In analyzing multiple variable relationships, parallel coordinate plots are a powerful tool that can provide valuable insights.

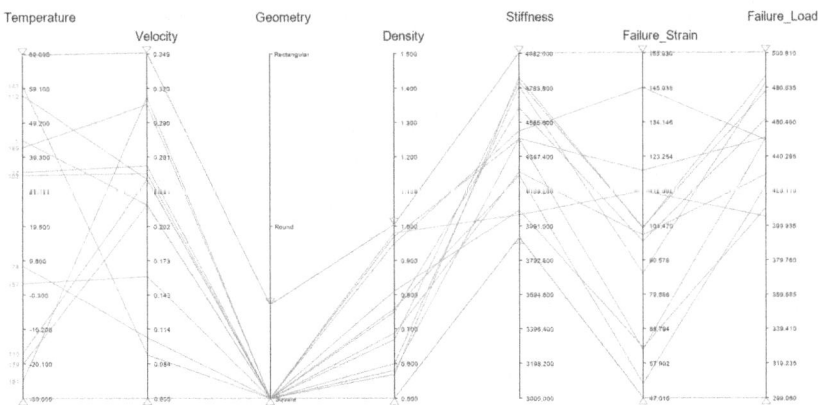

Figure 41: Parallel Coordinate Plot

- The Graph: The graph presented is a parallel coordinate plot, which allows us to visualize the relationships between multiple variables simultaneously.
- Geometry: The shape of the geometry appears to be a significant factor influencing the "Failure load." Specifically, for a "Square" shaped geometry, the "Failure load" tends to be high.

- Density: Lower densities are associated with higher "Failure load" values. This suggests that as density decreases, the ability to withstand failure increases.
- Stiffness: Higher stiffness values are also linked to higher "Failure load." This implies that materials with greater stiffness exhibit better resistance to failure.
- Temperature and Velocity: The distribution of "Temperature" and "Velocity" variables appears to have minimal impact on the "Failure load." These variables do not show a clear relationship with the outcome.

Parallel coordinate plots excel at capturing such insights by visualizing multiple variables and their relationships. The plot allows us to identify the key factors influencing the "Failure load" and understand the relative importance of different variables.

Overall, the parallel coordinate plot effectively conveys the relationships between variables and their impact on the "Failure load" in the depicted hypothetical dataset.

Exercises

You can use the support of Google or generative AI tools such as ChatGPT or Gemini to complete these exercises.

1. Exploratory vs. Explanatory Analysis in Retail Sales Data:
   Question: Using a Tableau Public dataset on retail sales, identify patterns of seasonal sales over the last five years. First, perform exploratory analysis to discover these patterns, then switch to explanatory analysis to present your findings on which quarters consistently perform best or worst. What visualization techniques aid in each phase of your analysis?

2. Context of Visualization in Global Smartphone Market Share:
   Question: Find a Tableau Public visualization showing the global smartphone market share. How does the context (historical trends, market competition, etc.) enhance the understanding of shifts in market dominance among companies? Discuss how background information and data annotation in the visualization contribute to this context.

3. Treemap Utilization in Fortune 500 Companies' Profitability:
   Question: Locate a treemap visualization on Tableau Public that represents the profitability of Fortune 500 companies. How does the treemap facilitate the comparison of profitability across different sectors? Explain how the size and color of the treemap provide insights into sector performance and individual company rankings within those sectors.

4. Dot Plots for Employee Satisfaction Surveys Across Industries:
   Question: Using a dot plot visualization from Tableau Public based on employee satisfaction surveys across various industries, analyze which factors contribute most to employee satisfaction. How do dot plots help in comparing these factors across industries, and what insights can you draw about industry-specific satisfaction drivers?

5. Bubble Chart Analysis of Global CO2 Emissions by Country:
   Question: Examine a bubble chart on Tableau Public that shows global CO2 emissions by country. How does the bubble chart's use of bubble size and color aid in highlighting the biggest contributors to CO2 emissions? Discuss the effectiveness of bubble charts in conveying the magnitude of emissions relative to country size or population.

CHAPTER 4

NAVIGATING THE VISUALIZATION PROJECT – STEPS AND CONSIDERATIONS

*U*nderstanding the business is crucial in projects related to Data warehousing, BI, Data Science, or Data Visualization. Without a strong understanding of the business, the entire project and analytics may veer in the wrong direction. To achieve effective analytics or visualization solutions, a deep comprehension of the business and how information can facilitate effective decision-making and enforce controls is essential. A "one size fits all" approach to visualization projects will not yield satisfactory results, as every business has unique aspects that require specific attention and have varying expectations.

Different organizations employ different approaches to understand business requirements, and there is no standard method. Although the methods may vary, the objective remains the same—to capture business requirements in a way that defines performance metrics. This exercise, which captures business requirements, can be referred to as business scoping, project charter, scope definition, or requirement gathering.

The timing of this exercise can also differ, with some organizations performing it after signing the contract while others do it as a pre-sales activity. Customers may use their internal resources or hire a consultant to perform the business scoping activity to help prepare RFIs or RFQs (Request for Information or Request for Quotation) from selected solution providers or to gather responses from the open market. The time required to capture business requirements may vary depending on the nature, size, and budget of the project. In complex business scenarios, the customer or their team may lack a complete understanding of all the intricacies involved, making it important to have workshops where the customer team, external consultants, and solution providers can brainstorm, discuss, and capture high-level business requirements that will evolve into detailed ones.

Business Scoping: Defining the Project Scope

The Business Scoping document becomes the foundation for understanding between the customer and the solution provider for all the data visualizations that will be delivered. This document sets the stage for defining SMART goals, project objectives, project deliverables, and project closure. Detailed business understanding is crucial for any visualization project, and it needs to be documented in a structured manner for knowledge sharing, knowledge transfer, or consumption by other stakeholders. Key deliverables and what needs to be done must be captured with precision and terminology that can be understood by the customer organization, solution provider, and other external consultants. Gathering important artifacts, diagrams, sample files, specification documents, and reports is also part of this exercise to facilitate exploratory analytics and visualization development. The following steps serve as a guideline, and additional steps may be included or excluded as needed:

- Business Capturing Strategy: Determine whether business scoping will be done internally, by external consultants, or by the solution provider.

Decide when this will be done—prior to starting the project, after project commencement, or as a separate project focused on business analysis. Allocate a budget and form a team accordingly.

- High-level business information: Gather an introduction to the business, information about the products or services they deal with, revenue details, and management team information.
- Prepare questionnaire: Use the high-level business information to create a structured questionnaire that raises additional queries.
- High-level visualization or analytics objective: Provide an overview of the business needs in relation to the project and the specific business need that the project aims to address. Capture any language customization or special objectives.
- Project Objectives: Define quantifiable goals in terms of time, money, and technical quality that the project must achieve to be considered successful. Refer to SMART goals discussed in previous chapters to ensure objectivity.
- Document Assumptions: Describe all assumptions and constraints considered.
- Document Scope Management Plan: Outline how project scope will be managed and how agreed-upon changes will be incorporated into the project deliverables. Include the change control process in this plan.
- Define Roles and Responsibilities: Establish the team structure and distribute tasks and responsibilities.
- Conduct Workshops or Discussions: Set an agenda, prepare the questionnaire, and organize workshops to capture detailed business requirements.
- Conduct Gap Analysis: Analyze existing dashboards or reports the customer may already have and determine if they can be reused, migrated, or discarded. Document the current KPIs versus the required KPIs.

- Understand overall performance expectations: If the customer has an existing solution, ensure a thorough understanding of its business scope. The new solution should always outperform the existing one.
- Complete Business Scoping and Sign-off.

In general, the solution provider or project team should strive to capture maximum business understanding, domain-specific knowledge, and supporting information that will aid the project during the exploratory phase and the creation of a detailed project plan.

Stages in Business Scoping: A Roadmap for Successful Projects

When dealing with a large and complex solution or analytics project, the business scoping exercise may require several days or weeks to complete. To meet customer expectations, it is important to provide a project plan or schedule specifically for the business scoping exercise. Below is an indicative business scoping schedule:

- Day 1:
  - Introduce the solution provider, customer, and the business
  - Capture high-level business information
  - Prepare the questionnaire

- Day 2: Workshop/Meeting with Business
  - Discuss business expectations
  - Gather reporting requirements
  - Identify critical areas to be prioritized
  - Understand existing processes

- Day 3: Meeting with the existing BI, DWH or Reporting team
  - Collect relevant information about existing systems
  - Obtain specifications and samples
  - Understand data formats and standards

- Discuss data acquisition and transfer methods
- Address integration and migration considerations

- Day 5: Meeting with the IT team
  - Discuss data volume, hardware, and other IT environments (e.g., OS, security, allowed software)
  - Address data transfer requirements

- Day 6: Consolidate the gathered information into the scope document

- Day 7: Discussion with the business on high-level analytics or performance metrics to be delivered

- Day 11: Finalize the scope document
  - Present the final scope to the stakeholders
  - Submit the scope document for sign-off

- Day 12: Obtain sign-off on the final scope.

It is important to note that this schedule serves as a general guideline, and the duration of each phase may vary based on the complexity of the project and the availability of resources. Adjustments can be made to accommodate specific project requirements and ensure a thorough and comprehensive business scoping exercise. After completing the business scoping exercise, development and remaining engineering tasks will be performed till the solution goes live.

Data Sources: Understanding and Selecting Relevant Data

A data source refers to the location, network element, or device where data is generated or digitized. Data can be generated in various formats, and extracting and utilizing it for analytics and visualization may require complex programming. In some cases, the data source owner or manufacturer may need to provide specifications or documentation to decode the data file. For example, ASN.1 is a telecom network standard file that requires the source provider's grammar to decode. Other examples include social media conversations (e.g., Twitter, Facebook), which require API documentation, and banking databases that capture ATM cash withdrawals and may have security-related complexities. Data sources can include databases, SS7 signals, flat files, live recordings, audio/video devices, scraped web data, or any system or source that generates and holds data.

Different File Formats

Data sources generate files in various formats, each with its own challenges and complexities when it comes to analytics and visualization. File formats should be chosen to ensure easy sharing, long-term access, and data preservation. It is important to select open standards and formats that are easy to reuse.

There may be situations where the data source undergoes upgrades or migrations, resulting in changes to the file format. In such cases, the data source owner must provide proper documentation about the changes, which should be maintained by the analytics team.

The analytics or visualization team should be equipped to work with different file formats and develop the capability to handle them. Here is a list of widely known file formats:

- Text: XML, PDF, HTML, Excel, Plain Text
- Binaries: ASN.1, Fixed Length
- Database: XML, CSV, TAB
- Still Image: TIFF, PNG, JPEG, BMP, GIF
- Geospatial: Shapefile (SHP, DBF, SHX), GeoTIFF, NetCDF
- Audio: WAVE, AIFF, MP3, MXF, FLAC
- Video: MOV, MPEG-4, AVI, MXF

Having proficiency in working with different file formats allows the analytics or visualization team to handle diverse data sources effectively.

Examples of File Formats

Below is a screengrab of a fixed-length binary file format:

```
00000000h: 42 5A 68 39 31 41 59 26 53 59 6F DC 02 C2 02 A3 ; BZh91AY&SYoÜ.Â.£
00000010h: 32 FF FF FF FF FF FF FF FF FF FF FF FF FF FF FF ; 2ÿÿÿÿÿÿÿÿÿÿÿÿÿÿÿ
00000020h: FF FF FF FF FF FF FF FF FF FF FF FF FF FF FF FF ; ÿÿÿÿÿÿÿÿÿÿÿÿÿÿÿÿ
00000030h: FF FF FF E1 B8 20 30 C8 0F BC 00 00 00 00 00 00 ; ÿÿÿá¸ 0È.¼.....
00000040h: 00 FB 3E 7A A5 46 DA 94 55 36 CC 3D EC 7A 18 7C ; .û>z¥FÚ"U6Ì=ìz.|
00000050h: 00 00 00 F9 00 00 00 00 00 00 00 00 00 00 00 00 ; ...ù...........
00000060h: 00 00 00 00 00 00 00 00 DC C0 00 0C F0 17 60 ; ........ÜÀ..ð.`
00000070h: 00 28 00 00 00 00 00 00 00 00 00 00 C6 3C AA ; .(..........Æ<ª
00000080h: 8D 3E 6E 3E A8 0A 0A 0A 00 0A 14 00 F1 00 D0 05 ; □>n>"......ñ.Ð.
00000090h: 9A 78 7B 56 36 58 16 97 7D 2A EC 70 AD 6B 61 66 ; šx{V6X.—}*ìp-kaf
000000a0h: 15 2B 29 20 00 36 AF AD 45 4A DA C1 23 80 F9 A7 ; .+) .6¯-EJÚÁ#€ù§
000000b0h: A7 1D 35 A2 74 7B BE 00 8F A8 00 00 00 10 06 01 ; §.5¢t{¾.□¨......
000000c0h: F0 DB 40 37 D2 9C FA D0 87 D3 D5 81 B5 A9 A2 61 ; ðÛ@7Òœú‡ÓÕ□µ©¢a
000000d0h: 9B 30 01 B1 A8 5D 60 23 00 07 92 80 00 00 15 4A ; ›0.±¨]`#..'€...J
000000e0h: 00 A1 40 00 75 54 A4 14 1D 28 F6 D4 2D 1B 61 9B ; .¡@.uT¤..(öÔ-.a›
000000f0h: 62 0A D0 03 B9 80 A1 40 48 EE B3 A9 37 61 A5 BB ; b.Ð.¹€¡@Hî³©7a¥»
00000100h: BA A9 DB 55 2A AB 5B 52 D5 55 B6 F0 00 01 8F 59 ; º©ÛU*«[RÕU¶ð..□Y
00000110h: 03 AC 16 D6 05 73 86 98 ED D0 00 00 00 D0 A0 ; .¬.Ö.s†˜íÐ....Ð
00000120h: 00 00 0A 1A 53 20 00 01 6E 55 C9 A0 60 39 00 01 ; ....S ..nUÉ `9..
00000130h: 9C 00 25 77 0A 00 00 A0 00 00 00 28 0A 00 34 1A ; œ.%w... ...(..4.
00000140h: 00 03 51 9E ED 00 00 77 80 00 00 F7 3D CC 00 01 ; ..Qží..w€..÷=Ì..
00000150h: A0 00 2A 9E 80 00 00 03 42 80 00 0A 00 00 04 DB ; .*ž€...B€.....Û
00000160h: C8 00 00 1B 6E 80 00 00 01 D9 80 01 4D 00 00 D0 ; È...n€...Ù€.M..Ð
00000170h: 01 40 05 00 00 16 EE 00 00 3B BD B8 00 00 00 00 ; .@....î..;½¸....
00000180h: 00 00 00 00 00 00 00 06 1D 97 60 00 03 C8 03 25 ; .........—`..È.%
00000190h: 24 00 50 00 00 A0 50 00 02 E0 00 45 B4 69 9A D9 ; $.P.. P..à.E´išÙ
000001a0h: 98 00 02 6D B6 CC B6 9A 00 00 06 20 00 54 C9 7A ; ˜..m¶Ì¶š... .TÉz
000001b0h: 6B 6C 00 DD CE BB 71 D9 45 74 6B 4C EB 36 6B B8 77 ; klÝÎ»qÙEtkLë6k¸w
000001c0h: 55 2E 43 6D 8E 00 03 74 E4 95 52 4B 76 D0 14 07 ; U.CmŽ..tä•RKvÐ..
000001d0h: 43 B8 CD C7 03 A6 E0 74 00 00 00 01 A3 D0 00 00 ; C¸ÍÇ.¦àt....£Ð..
000001e0h: 6D B4 0A 00 00 00 00 00 02 80 00 00 00 00 00 D0 ; m´......€......Ð
000001f0h: 00 00 77 81 60 00 00 00 00 00 14 00 F4 00 00 16 ; ..w□`.......ô...
00000200h: C0 00 D3 B6 F4 00 00 17 B0 00 00 0E CF 6E 09 00 ; À.Ó¶ô...°...Ïn..
00000210h: 00 01 40 00 05 0B 1C 0D 00 00 A0 00 32 00 05 00 ; ..@....... .2...
00000220h: 34 50 18 10 9C 0E 80 15 40 00 F6 F7 90 57 7A 01 ; 4P..œ.€.@.ö÷□Wz.
00000230h: 40 28 F2 03 D0 BD DE C4 0C 20 01 EE 20 0C EA DA ; @(ò.Ð½ÞÄ. .î .êÚ
```

Figure 42: Fixed Length Binary

Below is a screengrab of ASN.1 file format:

```
00 FF E1 81 B3 C2 01 04 C3 01 1D FF 27 11 C6 08
14 09 23 00 10 15 72 F0 C7 05 69 65 38 49 96 ED
10 D3 03 05 01 07 F4 05 DC 03 05 30 02 D1 02 00
02 DF 2C 0D 81 ED 0F FF FF FF FF FF FF FF FF FF
FF CA 02 84 DC FB 0D 16 06 41 55 49 52 30 30 D0
03 00 00 00 DE 09 41 44 33 32 30 4C 37 30 31 FF
21 0D 16 06 4D 54 43 30 31 42 D0 03 00 25 0F DF
30 03 3F E3 0E F7 06 FF 2B 03 C9 01 2B DF 20 05
A1 69 04 63 F3 DF 2F 01 02 DF 52 01 02 DF 53 02
00 7F DF 54 01 01 DF 55 02 00 00 FF 46 16 DF 47
03 81 ED 0F DF 49 03 05 30 02 DF 4A 03 05 01 07
DF 4B 01 02 DF 3B 01 01 E1 81 B6 C2 01 04 C3 01
01 FF 27 1B C6 08 14 09 13 00 01 54 94 F8 C7 05
69 65 23 40 91 C8 08 53 33 85 00 25 49 85 01 ED
10 D3 03 05 01 07 F4 05 DC 03 05 28 51 D1 02 00
49 C5 01 00 DF 2C 0D 81 36 02 07 F1 FF FF FF FF
FF FF FF FF CA 02 84 DC CB 02 02 3C CC 01 11 CF
01 05 FB 0D 16 06 4D 49 43 4F 55 54 D0 03 00 00
00 D5 03 30 18 81 D6 07 14 F9 30 88 13 D7 17 DE
09 41 44 33 32 30 4C 37 30 31 FF 21 0D 16 06 4A
```

Figure 43: ASN.1

Below is a screengrab of the text file:

```
Buyer,Month,Style,Season,LotSize,Reject%
C&A CANDA,14-Apr,LADIES,SS14,37853,0.49%
C&A CANDA,14-Apr,LADIES,SS14,19157,0.55%
C&A CANDA,14-Apr,LADIES,SS14,43423,0%
C&A CANDA,14-Apr,LADIES,SS14,31256,0.45%
C&A CANDA,14-Apr,LADIES,SS14,19704,0.99%
C&A YESSICA,14-Apr,LADIES,SS14,33447,0.61%
C&A YESSICA,14-Apr,LADIES,SS14,22617,0.69%
C&A YESSICA,14-Apr,LADIES,SS14,10078,0.49%
C&A YESSICA,14-Apr,LADIES,SS14,2113,1.51%
C&A YESSICA,14-Apr,LADIES,SS14,44400,0.19%
C&A YESSICA,14-Apr,LADIES,SS14,34663,1.10%
C&A YESSICA,14-Apr,LADIES,SS14,36112,1.03%
C&A YESSICA,14-Apr,LADIES,SS14,49913,0.67%
C&A YESSICA,14-Apr,LADIES,SS14,37082,1.19%
C&A YESSICA,14-Apr,LADIES,SS14,34646,1.28%
C&A YESSICA,14-Apr,LADIES,SS14,27312,1.87%
C&A YESSICA,14-Apr,LADIES,SS14,16246,1.28%
```

Figure 44: Text File

Below is a screengrab of the JSON object:

```
{
    name: "DCIM",
    type: "folder",
    path: "DCIM",
    items: [
        {
            name: "Snaphots",
            type: "folder",
            path: "DCIM/Snaphots",
            items: [ ]
        },
        {
            name: "SoundRecorder",
            type: "folder",
            path: "DCIM/SoundRecorder",
            items: [ ]
        },
        {
            name: "VideoRecorder",
            type: "folder",
            path: "DCIM/VideoRecorder",
            items: [
                {
                    name: "2018-03-06_13.36.mov",
                    type: "file",
                    path: "DCIM/VideoRecorder/2018-03-06_13.36.mov",
                    size: 40351122
```

Figure 45: JSON

Below is an example of a still image:

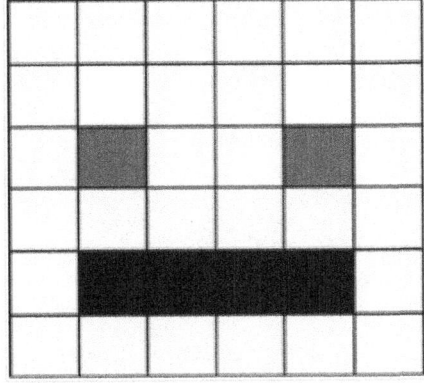

Figure 46: Still Image

Two bits are used to store the following colors:

00 – White; 01 – Black; 10 – Yellow; 11 – Blue

In order for the computer to interpret the image, the computer needs to know the following:

- Color depth – how many bits represent each pixel
- Resolution - Width & Height (in pixels)

Below is how the bits are arranged to provide the image, and a similar approach works for all binaries to text geospatial or videos.

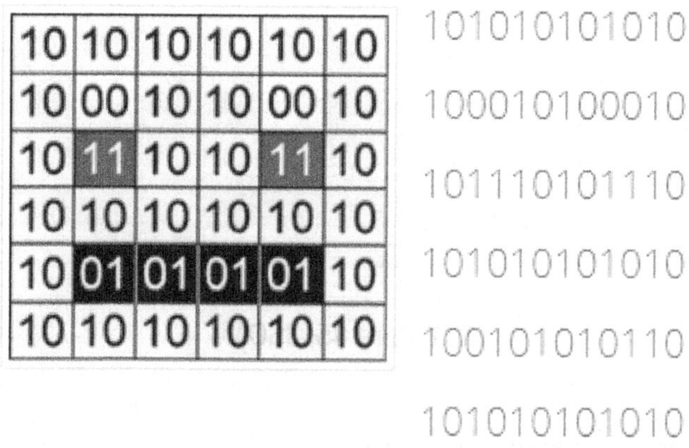

10	10	10	10	10	10
10	00	10	10	00	10
10	11	10	10	11	10
10	10	10	10	10	10
10	01	01	01	01	10
10	10	10	10	10	10

101010101010
100010100010
101110101110
101010101010
100101010110
101010101010

Figure 47: Colors

Below is an example of a shapefile and how it is represented in map view:

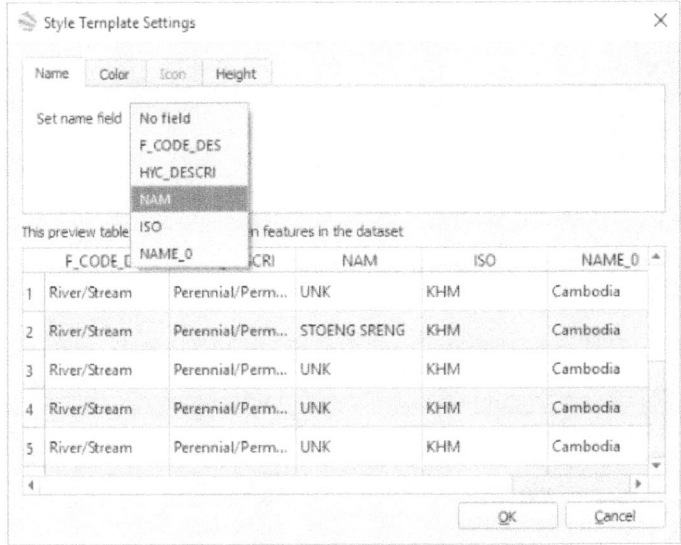

Figure 48: Mapview Data

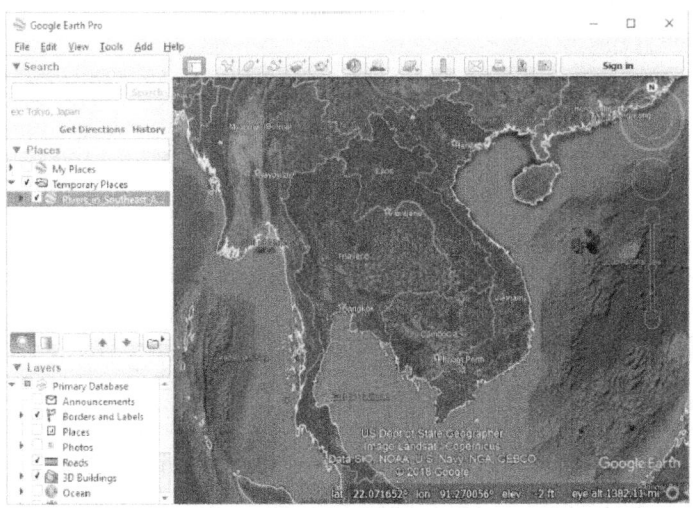

Figure 49: Map
(Source: https://www.google.com/earth/outreach/learn/
importing-geographic-information-systems-gis-data-in-google-earth/)

Below is an example of a scanned image; we apply OCR to this image to extract details of the invoice:

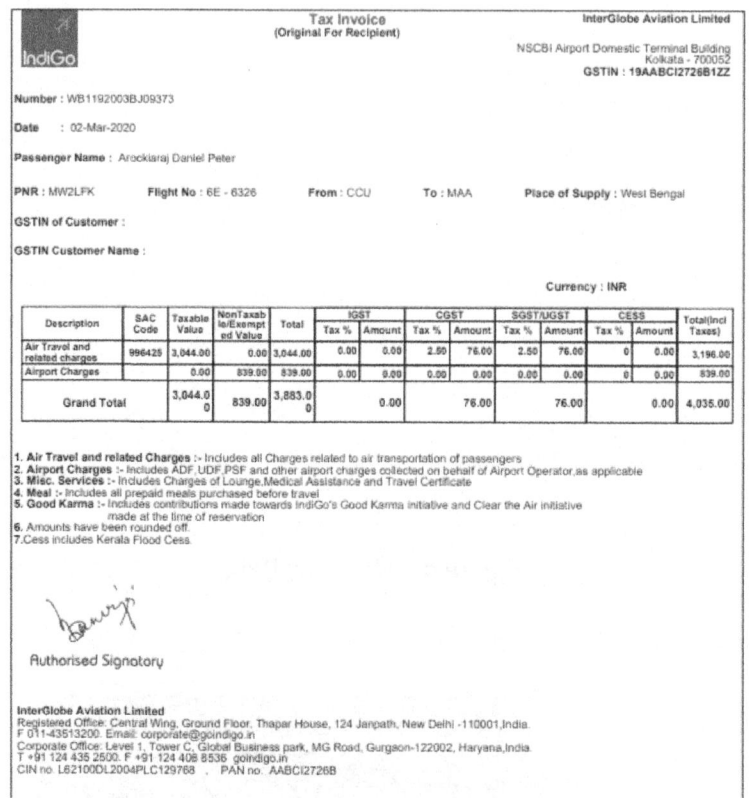

Figure 50: OCR

Data Acquisition: Collecting and Preparing Data for Visualization

Data acquisition refers to the process of acquiring, extracting, or collecting data from various data sources. The acquired data is then further processed, enriched, and utilized for analytics and visualization purposes. The objective of data acquisition is to retrieve the required data from the source system with minimal resources, making it the initial technical step in an analytics or visualization project. It is worth noting that data acquisition and the transfer mode are often discussed during the business scoping phase. In many cases, customers transfer the data, and the transferred data is considered acquired by the analytics project.

The different modes of data transfer and acquisition widely used are:

- FTP (File Transfer Protocol): FTP is designed for both single file and bulk file transfers. However, it is not as strong in terms of security.
- FTPS (FTP over SSL): FTPS includes data-in-motion encryption, as well as server and client authentication, providing a higher level of security.
- SFTP (Secure File Transfer Protocol): SFTP runs on SSH (Secure Shell), which is a secure protocol similar to SSL. It supports data-in-motion encryption and client/server authentication. SFTP is more firewall-friendly compared to FTPS.
- HTTP: HTTP is easy to implement and useful for person-to-server and person-to-person file transfers. It is also less prone to firewall issues.
- API (Application Programming Interface): Data Transfer API manages the transfer of data from one user to another within a domain. An API must be defined for the transfer and may include application-specific parameters.

By utilizing these different data transfer and acquisition modes, organizations can efficiently collect the required data for their analytics and visualization projects.

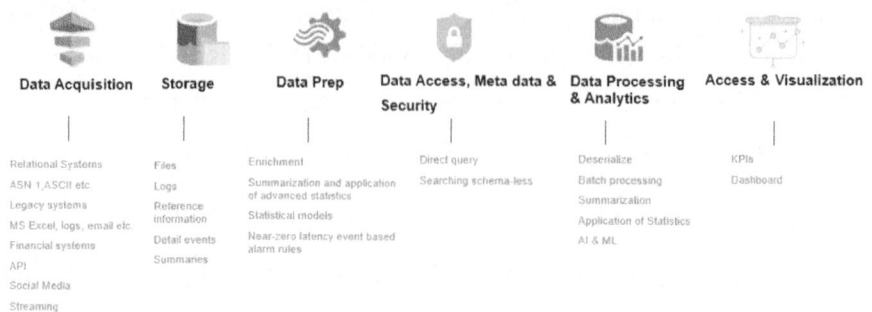

Figure 51: Visualization Process Flow

Defining Business Logic from Data

Business logic plays a crucial role in translating business understanding into Key Performance Indicators (KPIs) in data analytics projects. For instance, when dealing with complex telecom Call Detail Records (CDRs) that contain numerous fields, the business logic determines how the data should be enriched, filtered, and summarized to calculate a simple KPI like total call duration per day.

Business logic is responsible for defining the necessary data transformations, aggregations, and filtering conditions to derive the desired KPIs. It can be documented in a straightforward manner using layman's terms, arithmetic formulas, explanatory descriptions, SQL syntax, or other programming syntax that is understandable to all stakeholders involved. The defined business logic will be implemented in the analytics program to generate visualizations that meet the specific requirements of the business.

By effectively defining and applying business logic, organizations can ensure that the data is processed in a way that aligns with their business objectives, allowing for meaningful insights and informed decision-making.

Example of Business Logic:

In the case of a customer providing paid sports news through a mobile app, business logic would be employed to determine various key metrics and calculations related to the app's subscriptions and revenue. Here is an example of how business logic could be applied

Business Requirement

- Find monthly ARPU (Average Revenue Per User)
- Find monthly ARPS (Average Revenue Per Subscription)

Data Sources

Subscription Table. Below is the table schema

txn_ID	created_at	subscriber_ID	amount_USD
19696054	4/14/2020	2064958619	100
19696052	4/14/2020	2068146159	100
19696051	4/14/2020	2064505269	500
19696019	4/14/2020	2065033871	100
19696018	4/14/2020	2069121186	500
19696017	4/14/2020	2066751190	100
19696016	4/14/2020	2069594819	100
19695989	4/14/2020	2069490593	0
19695988	4/14/2020	2065014628	500
19695986	4/14/2020	2066720662	100

Figure 52: Subscription Table Schema Sample

Logic

- Monthly ARPU
  - Filter in data for the relevant month
  - SUM(amount_USD)
  - Find distinct Subscriber_ID for the month

- ○ SUM(amount_USD) / count distinct Subscriber_ID for the month
- Monthly ARPS
  - ○ Filter in data for the relevant month
  - ○ SUM(amount_USD)
  - ○ Count(txn_ID)
  - ○ SUM(amount_USD) / Count (txn_ID) for the month

The above example provides a basic table schema and the business logic required to populate the KPI. There could be complex scenarios where an SQL syntax may help instead of writing a generic step like the above. SQL syntax would look like below for the month of April 2020 for Monthly ARPS:

"Select month(created_at), year(created_at), sum(amount_USD)/count(1) as "Monthly_ARPS") where month(created_at) = 4, year(created_at) = 2020 group by month(created_at), year(created_at)"

Business logic must explain the business requirement for the KPI, the schema of the transformed data table and the logic to summarize or create a model.

Challenges & Constraints

Every project, including software development and analytics projects, has its own set of constraints and challenges. In addition to general project management constraints, there are specific constraints that are important to consider in the context of understanding requirements and defining logic. These constraints can impact the success of the project. Some of these constraints include:

- Lack of management commitment: When project stakeholders or management are not fully committed to the project, it can lead to delays, lack of resources, and reduced support.

- Lost sponsor: If the project sponsor or key decision-maker is no longer involved or changes within the organization, it can create challenges in obtaining necessary approvals and guidance.
- Lack of business participation: Involvement and input from business stakeholders are crucial for understanding requirements accurately. If there is a lack of participation, it can result in misunderstandings and ineffective solutions.
- Imposed, unrealistic schedule: When project timelines are imposed without considering the complexity of the requirements, it can lead to rushed and suboptimal outcomes.
- Unrealistic scope for the schedule: If the scope of work is not properly defined and aligned with the project schedule, it can lead to scope creep and difficulties in meeting deadlines.
- Unrealistic expectations: When project expectations are set unrealistically high or are not aligned with the available resources, it can result in dissatisfaction and project failure.
- Unrealistic budget: Insufficient budget allocation can restrict the resources and capabilities needed to successfully complete the project.
- Untrained or unavailable staff: Inadequate skill sets or unavailability of skilled staff can hinder the project's progress and impact the quality of deliverables.
- Constantly changing business priorities: Shifting business priorities can introduce uncertainty and frequent changes in project requirements, making it challenging to achieve project goals.
- Ineffective project management: Poor project management practices can result in inefficient communication, lack of coordination, and increased project risks.
- Limited scalability: If the project does not consider scalability requirements, it may face difficulties in accommodating future growth and expansion.

Visualization Requirements

Gathering visualization requirements differs from defining business logic and can involve an iterative process due to its artistic nature. However, there are best practices that can help in outlining visualization requirements and reducing rework and iterations. Consider the following points:

- Understand the audience: Identify the target audience for the visualizations and their specific needs, preferences, and expertise. This understanding will help tailor the visualizations accordingly.
- Understand the context: Gain a deep understanding of the business context in which the visualizations will be used. Consider the industry, domain-specific requirements, and any relevant regulations or standards.
- Understand the level of detail: Determine the level of detail required in the visualizations. This could range from high-level summaries to granular insights, depending on the intended use and audience.
- Understand how much historical information has to be represented: Clarify whether the visualizations should focus on current data or include historical trends and patterns. This will influence the design and functionality of the visualizations.

By considering these points and involving stakeholders throughout the process, the visualization requirements can be effectively captured, leading to more successful and impactful visualizations in the final deliverables.

Audience Focus: Tailoring Visualization for Effective Communication

Understanding the audience is crucial when designing KPIs, reports, and dashboards to ensure effective communication of analytics without ambiguity. Visualization serves as a communication tool to convey business performance, operational insights, and other information supported by data. However, it is important to avoid providing complex information that may not be easily digestible for the intended audience.

Sometimes, amateur analysts make the mistake of designing dashboards based on their own preferences and knowledge rather than considering the needs and capabilities of the users. It is essential to prioritize audience-centric design and understand what information will be most useful and understandable for the intended users. While strong technical skills are valuable, it is the audience-centric approach that truly enables effective visualization.

In the process of designing dashboards, it is helpful to use storyboarding techniques. By creating a narrative or story that aligns with the audience's needs and interests, the dashboard can be structured to convey relevant and meaningful facts. Different stories can be told through various KPIs and reports included in the dashboard. These stories can focus on performance, future projections, customer perspectives, and more, depending on the audience's requirements.

Taking the example of a car's dashboard, it provides essential information in a way that allows the driver to safely navigate the journey by making necessary adjustments such as controlling speed, reducing acceleration, and refueling. Similarly, an analytics dashboard should aim to provide the right KPIs and information that are relevant and actionable for the audience rather than overwhelming them with excessive data.

In addition to traditional visual dashboards, AI-based textual reports are also gaining popularity. These reports are designed to be read like a blog or a news article, providing users with a narrative-driven experience that presents key insights and findings.

By keeping the audience at the forefront of dashboard design considering their needs, preferences, and understanding levels, analysts can create impactful visualizations that effectively communicate analytics and drive informed decision-making.

Sample Car Dashboard KPIs:

Figure 53: Car Dashboard

Speedometer

The speedometer reflects the speed of the vehicle and is measured using a transmission output shaft speed sensor. This data is then converted by the vehicle's computer using an algorithm to display the accurate speed. In the past, vehicles used a speedometer cable instead of a sensor.

Fuel Gauge

The fuel gauge indicates the amount of fuel remaining in the vehicle's tank for combustion. It is connected to a component within the tank, known as a "float," which literally floats in the gas tank. The needle on the gauge does not constantly move while the vehicle is in motion, as it utilizes a system that averages out the reading in real time, often displayed as a percentage

Tachometer

The tachometer displays the speed of the engine in revolutions per minute (RPM). It is particularly useful when towing a trailer or driving on steep grades. Tachometers are commonly found in vehicles with manual transmissions, helping the driver determine the optimal time to shift gears.

Water Temperature Gauge

This gauge communicates the temperature of the vehicle's engine coolant. While many vehicle dashboard gauges use analog needles to display an approximate temperature reading, some cars provide a live, digital display of the temperature.

Understanding the Context

When designing a dashboard, it is crucial to consider the audience and their specific needs. For example, providing a dashboard to an operations team differs from designing one for executives. Operations teams often require detailed operational insights, while executives focus on the big picture. Each report, KPI, or visual within the dashboard should provide the appropriate context for the presented facts and figures. It is important to include relevant benchmarks, comparative data, historical trends, and other contextual information, such as competitor performance or growth rates from previous periods.

Understanding the Level of Detail

Understanding the audience and the context also helps determine the level of detail to be included in the dashboard. For instance, if a fraud analyst is using the dashboard, it may be necessary to provide detailed information related to the initial transaction to aid in their investigation. On the other hand, the department head of the fraud investigation team may only require summary statistics. Additionally, the department head may need real-time insights, which can be provided faster than an analyst but without delving into intricate details.

By considering the audience, context, and level of detail, dashboard designers can create effective visuals that provide meaningful information and support decision-making.

Exercise

1. Data Visualization of Movie Streaming Platforms:
   a. Utilize the Movies dataset from Netflix, Prime Video, Hulu, and Disney+ available on Kaggle[3].
   b. Create a dashboard in Tableau showcasing the distribution of movies across these platforms.

2. Exploratory Data Analysis (EDA) on Coffee Chain Sales:
   a. Access the Sample-Superstore dataset in Tableau. Generate visualizations that analyze sales trends, regional performance, and product categories within the coffee chain dataset.

3. Analyzing Movie Ratings and Genres:
   a. Develop a visualization in Tableau that illustrates the relationship between movie genres and their ratings [3]

4. Customer Segmentation Based on Purchase Behavior:
   a. Employ the Sample-Superstore dataset in Tableau for customer segmentation analysis
   b. Create a dashboard that categorizes customers based on their purchase behavior and demographics.

5. Comparative Analysis of Movie Availability:
   a. Utilize the Movies dataset to compare movie availability across different streaming platforms.
   b. Design visualizations in Tableau that highlight the overlap and unique content offerings of Netflix, Prime Video, Hulu, and Disney+. [3]

These exercise questions leverage Kaggle datasets to practice data visualization, exploratory data analysis, and dashboard creation using Tableau.

Citations:

[1] https://www.kaggle.com/code/mahmoudhamza/tableau-study-guide

[2] https://www.youtube.com/watch?v=JwTGPsMgluw

[3] https://www.kaggle.com/code/ruchi798/movies-data-collection-eda-using-tableau

[4] https://community.tableau.com/s/question/0D54T00000C6YZhSAN/sample-data-sets-for-practice

6. **Student Learning Activity:** Scoping a Business Visualization Project

"EcoRetail Corp" is looking to enhance its decision-making processes by improving how it visualizes sales, customer, and inventory data. The company has data scattered across various systems and formats and requires a comprehensive dashboard that provides clear, actionable insights into its operations.

Task:

You are part of a project management team assigned to scope this visualization project. Your task is to define the project scope, including objectives, deliverables, and key milestones. You will also need to outline the data sources required and the types of visualizations that would best serve the company's needs.

Instructions:

1. Define Project Objectives: Identify the primary objectives EcoRetail Corp aims to achieve with this dashboard. Consider aspects such as increasing sales, improving inventory management, and enhancing customer satisfaction.
2. List Deliverables: Enumerate the specific deliverables your project will produce. This should include the final dashboard, any interim reports, and documentation on data sources and methodologies used.
3. Identify Data Sources: List the potential data sources that will need to be integrated into the dashboard. Consider sales records, customer feedback, inventory levels, and supplier data.
4. Select Visualization Types: Choose appropriate visualization types (e.g., treemaps for inventory categorization, dot plots for sales trends, bubble charts for customer demographics) that will meet the project objectives. Justify your choices based on the data type and the insights they could provide.
5. Outline Key Milestones: Develop a high-level timeline for the project, including key milestones such as data consolidation, initial dashboard design, user testing, and final deployment.

Deliverables:

Prepare a project scoping document that includes the following sections:
- Project Overview: A brief introduction to the project and its importance to EcoRetail Corp.
- Objectives: Detailed description of the project objectives.
- Deliverables: A comprehensive list of the project's deliverables.
- Data Sources: Identification and evaluation of required data sources.

- Visualization Types: A rationale for the chosen visualization types, including their relevance to the objectives.
- Milestones: A timeline with key milestones and their expected completion dates.

Evaluation Criteria:

- Completeness: All sections of the scoping document are thoroughly addressed.
- Coherence: The objectives, deliverables, and visualizations are logically aligned with the project's goals.
- Creativity: Innovative approaches to data visualization and problem-solving are demonstrated.
- Practicality: The scope is realistic and achievable within typical project constraints (time, budget, resources).

To complete this exercise effectively, utilize resources like Google or generative AI tools such as ChatGPT, Gemini or Claude for assistance. This activity aims to enhance your understanding of project scoping and underscore the importance of a well-defined plan in successful visualization project delivery.

CHAPTER 5

EXPLORING MODERN TOOLS FOR DATA VISUALIZATION

*B*efore the adoption of graphical user interfaces (GUI) in computers, the visualization community relied on manual methods to create charts and graphs using external tools outside the computer. As graphical user interfaces started to emerge, computer systems began to provide graphical tools for creating presentational graphs and charts, initially focusing on high-level summaries.

However, with the advancements in computers and business intelligence systems, such as net banking and mobile banking, which are strongly supported by robust data management systems and cloud-based architectures, visualization has gained even greater importance. The availability of high computing power, storage capabilities, processing capabilities, and display technologies has further propelled the field of data visualization. Additionally, modern software tools powered by programming tools have accelerated the pace of data visualization, with a growing trend towards "No Code" frameworks in the software world.

Data visualization tools now offer a wide range of capabilities, from simple pie graphs to interactive choropleths and attractive infographics.

With these powerful capabilities in the hands of visualization designers, organizations face the challenge of choosing the right visualization tool. This chapter aims to provide an overview of commercial and open-source software that is useful for creating high-quality data visualizations. It also explores how the world of data visualization is evolving towards self-service visualization, where users can create visualizations without extensive coding or technical expertise.

Factors Influencing Tool Selection: Considerations

- Inhouse server versus cloud applications
- Degree of customization
- Open source vs. Commercial software
- Data integration capability
- Data refresh capability
- Provision for real-time analytics
- Total cost of ownership

In-house Server vs. Cloud Applications

The choice between hosting the data visualization software in-house or in the cloud has its own set of advantages and disadvantages. When considering in-house server options, factors such as ease of installation, adoption hierarchy, licensing, and software maintenance should be considered. On the other hand, cloud applications offer ease of deployment, scalability, and reduced maintenance overhead. Assessing these factors will help determine the most suitable mode of hosting for the visualization software.

Table 7: Hosting In-house Vs Cloud

Factor	In-house Server	Cloud
Degree of customization	Low to High	Low to High
Ease of Installation	Easy to Hard and depends on the degree of customization	Usually Easy
Adoption	Hierarchical controls to be provided	individual user logins
Licensing	Server-hosted: Perpetual and Monthly	Cloud Hosted
Software maintenance	dedicated team in-house	remote support
Learning curve	Varies based on customization and features	Varies based on customization and features
Operating System	Mobile, Laptop, Desktop	Mobile, Laptop, Desktop

Degree of Customization

The degree of customization is a crucial criterion for selecting a visualization tool. Off-the-shelf packages generally provide a standard set of features that cater to a broad audience. However, if these standard features do not meet an organization's specific requirements, they can opt for a customized version of commercial or open-source software. It is important to note that customization comes with associated costs such as monetary investment, allocation of human resources, time, and uncertainty. The extent of customization required greatly influences the cost of the software.

In addition to customization, there are other factors to consider when selecting the right software. One often overlooked factor is the learning curve associated with using the software. Commercial software tends to excel in this aspect due to extensive documentation, including text documents, tutorial videos, and optional training programs tailored to individual organizations.

Data visualization software typically offers both standard visualizations and custom visualizations. Standard visualizations, such as histograms, pie charts, and line charts, can be created using built-in libraries available in the software. Even in user-friendly software, all visualizations are created using these built-in libraries. However, there may be cases where the standard visualizations do not meet an organization's requirements, leading to the need for custom visualizations. Custom visualizations allow users to create custom logic and query results, which are not part of the standard libraries. While standard visualizations are suitable for individuals or small businesses, large businesses and organizations often rely on custom visualizations.

It is important to note that what is considered a custom visualization today may become a standard visualization in the future, resulting in lower costs. The availability of standard versus custom visualization tools in a software package significantly impacts the total cost of the visualization software. If a software lacks custom visualization options, it tends to be cheaper. However, if businesses require custom visualization tools, additional costs arise due to the development of custom libraries that are not built in. Hence, the degree of customization required should be carefully considered when selecting a visualization tool.

Open Source vs. Commercial Software

Open-source software, available in the public domain with a free license, offers the advantage of a larger community for support. However, open-source software generally lacks clear documentation, tutorials, and certainty about future development and can have buggy feature releases. Some companies also use open-source tools as bait to sell licensed versions. Open-source software often covers a wide range of visualization features that may not be available even in commercial software. However, the organization's skill set and technical know-how in utilizing open-source software play an important role in the decision-making process.

On the other hand, commercial software excels in providing professional presentations and offers extensive user support, clear documentation, and professional services. These features make commercial software preferable for professional presentations and applications.

Data Integration Capabilities

Data integration capabilities of visualization software are crucial requirements during the selection process. Regardless of the type of visualization software, all of them require some level of data integration capabilities. Organizations can import data from various sources, such as basic software like MS Excel, SQL databases, OLAP engines, or big data tools like Kafka, HDFS, Hive, Impala, and more. However, a challenge faced by all data visualization software is the need to support numerous database software and file formats. This is where the adoption of data lake concepts becomes increasingly important to address these challenges in data integration capabilities. The solution diagram below represents a data lake where we can see source systems supplying data to the streaming engine all the way till visualization:

Exploring Modern Tools for Data Visualization

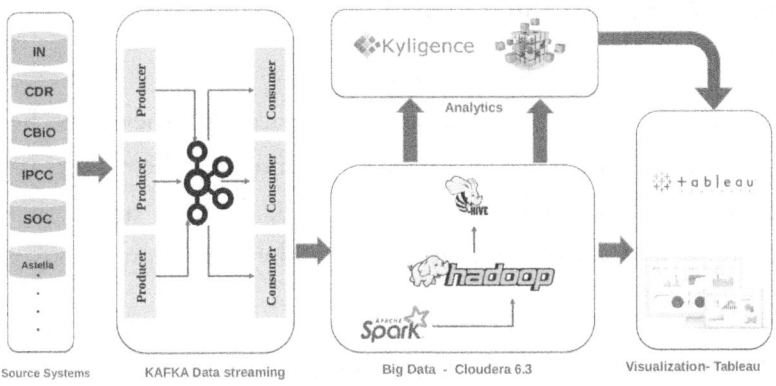

Figure 54: Architecture

Visualization software tools indeed face a challenge when dealing with unstructured data as compared to structured data. The requirements for analyzing unstructured data became prominent with the rise of the Internet and social media platforms. Nowadays, organizations not only rely on their ERP systems or similar tools for data analysis but also extensively scrape data from social media platforms like Twitter, Instagram, and Facebook.

Unstructured data poses difficulties because it requires significant efforts in terms of data processing and cleansing. Each organization may have different requirements and approaches for handling and extracting insights from unstructured data. This variability adds complexity to the visualization process.

To address these challenges, data aggregators have emerged in the market. They provide data-as-a-service with a certain level of enrichment to social media data. These aggregators help businesses by collecting and processing unstructured data from various sources, making it more accessible and usable for analysis and visualization purposes.

Overall, while visualization software tools excel in handling structured data, the analysis and visualization of unstructured data, such as social media data, require additional efforts and specialized techniques due to its inherent complexity and variability.

Businesses often have legacy systems in place that they have heavily invested in. As a result, they seek ways to integrate these systems with their existing data warehouses. By doing so, they can utilize the data stored in their legacy systems for analysis and visualization purposes.

In some cases, the existing data warehouse is capable of handling part of the data extraction and loading operations needed for visualization. This means that businesses can leverage their current infrastructure instead of investing in a completely new data warehouse. However, there are situations where a new data warehouse is necessary to meet the specific requirements of data visualization.

Fortunately, the field of data management has evolved significantly to address integration needs for both individuals and organizations. There are now robust data integration tools and technologies available that facilitate smooth data movement, transformation, and synchronization across different systems. These tools enable businesses to seamlessly connect their visualization software with their existing data warehouses, ensuring a seamless flow of data for analysis and visualization.

By leveraging these data integration capabilities, businesses can maximize the value of their legacy systems while harnessing the power of visualization software to gain valuable insights from their data.

Data Refresh Capability and Real-time Analytics:

In today's data-driven landscape, both data refresh capability and real-time analytics play crucial roles in enabling organizations to make timely and informed decisions.

Data Refresh Capability refers to the ability of visualization software to provide users with the latest analytics at specified intervals. Higher data refresh capabilities allow for more real-time analysis, empowering organizations to leverage up-to-date insights. However, it is important to consider that higher data refresh capabilities often come with a cost that organizations need to be prepared to invest in. The data refresh process relies on factors like solution architecture, design, data modeling, and hardware resources. Advanced techniques such as counters, vector processing, and in-memory processing have been developed to support real-time analytics. Some systems adopt a hybrid approach, combining real-time and batch processing to optimize hardware resource utilization.

Real-time Analytics, on the other hand, has gained prominence due to affordable storage and computation, improved processing capabilities, and increasing consumer demands. Organizations can now access real-time data from various departments across the enterprise, facilitating timely decision-making. Advancements in streaming pipeline tools, vector processing, and in-memory databases have made real-time analytics a reality. Machine Learning and Artificial Intelligence models further enhance real-time alerts and predictive scenarios, enabling organizations to overcome technical challenges associated with real-time data analysis.

By incorporating data refresh capability and real-time analytics into their visualization software, businesses can access up-to-date insights, make faster data-driven decisions, and stay competitive in today's dynamic business environment.

Total Cost of Ownership (TCO)

While considering the decision-making factors discussed earlier, it is essential to also assess the financial aspect of the visualization project. The financial aspect can significantly influence the evaluation of the factors discussed thus far. In many cases, organizations may have extensive requirements, but management may allocate a limited budget for the visualization project. Evaluating all the factors helps prioritize features and scope while ensuring optimal outcomes within the project's financial constraints. By carefully managing the Total Cost of Ownership (TCO), organizations can strike a balance between their visualization needs and budgetary considerations. Below is a sample TCO calculator that's widely used in the industry, and this also helps understand the return on investment from the analytics:

Table 8: TCO Calculator

Item	Cost
Hardware / Cloud Storage	
Software License / Subscription	
External Resource	
Internal Resource	
Training	
Onsite Expenses	
Maintenance & Support	
Total	

We can generate estimates for the best-case, median-case, and worst-case scenarios regarding costs. These estimates can be calculated for a period of 3 or 5 years to determine the Total Cost of Ownership (TCO).

Tools Available in the Market: Overview of Visualization Tool Options

The landscape of data visualization software is vast, with hundreds of companies offering solutions tailored to various organizational needs. Each software tool exhibits significant variation across the factors specified in Table 7. As our book has limitations in terms of tool coverage, we present a concise list of visualization software that we deem important. For each listed tool, we provide detailed descriptions of their features to the best of our knowledge. For more comprehensive information, please refer to the official websites of the respective software.

Sisense

Sisense is a cloud-based application that serves as both a middleware and a front-end application. It enables the combination of various data outputs, allowing for the generation of comprehensive progress reports. With Sisense, it is possible to integrate multiple data feeds such as Google Analytics, Salesforce, call tracking, and internal systems specific to the company. Additionally, Sisense offers the unique capability to build data cubes, although there may be a slight learning curve for new users.

Unique Features of Sisense

- A wide variety of data sources
- Easy dashboard creation and collaboration
- Compatible with both Windows and Linux platforms

Tableau

Tableau stands out as one of the most popular and extensively used data visualization tools available today. With its broad range of interfaces compatible with virtually any database, Tableau offers exceptional versatility in terms of visualization capabilities. While primarily a commercial software, Tableau also offers alternative versions, including Tableau Public and academic licenses for the teaching community.

Tableau Public provides a free platform where users can create data visualizations without the need for any installation. However, it is important to note that Tableau Public visualizations are accessible to the entire Tableau community and the general public, making privacy a key consideration.

When comparing Tableau Desktop (TD) and Tableau Public (TP), there are a few notable differences:
- Privacy: Tableau Desktop offers greater privacy control, as it is not accessible to the general public.
- Visualization Tools: Tableau Desktop boasts a more extensive feature set compared to Tableau Public, providing users with advanced visualization capabilities.
- Data Sources: Tableau Desktop offers numerous integration options, enabling both read and write access to a wide range of databases.

Unique Features of Tableau

- Wide variety of data sources: Tableau supports seamless integration with diverse data sources, ensuring flexibility in accessing and analyzing data.
- Flexible dashboard building: Tableau provides a user-friendly interface for creating interactive and customizable dashboards, empowering users to effectively present their data.
- Professional quality graphs: With Tableau, users can generate visually stunning and professional-quality graphs, charts, and visualizations.
- Secure sharing and collaboration: Tableau facilitates secure sharing and collaboration on visualizations, allowing teams to work together efficiently and share insights across the organization.

iDashboards

iDashboards is a popular software in the visualization community, known for its extensive range of easily implementable chart templates. It offers various chart creation options and seamless integration with databases. Users find it user-friendly with a short learning curve.

Key features of iDashboards include integration with CRM and ERP tools, creating visualizations without programming knowledge, and on-demand or scheduled reporting solutions. It also provides a public access license for sharing visualizations with clients. While not mobile-editable, it offers on-demand report access through mobile apps.

iDashboards offers flexibility in creating dashboards to monitor KPIs, aiding strategic decision-making. Video resources on the official website assist new users.

Unique Features of iDashboards

- Easy data prep
- Drag and drop
- Incorporate apps
- Unlimited design options

Microsoft Power BI

Microsoft Power BI is a leading visualization software known for its extensive capabilities. As one of the oldest and most evolved software in the market, Power BI is highly favored by big organizations and boasts a large user community. It offers seamless integration with Microsoft products like Azure and Access, enabling comprehensive data integration and analytics. Additionally, it provides direct integration with the Bloomberg database for market data procurement.

Power BI supports API integration for retrieving user information across various assets such as reports, dashboards, datasets, dataflows, workspaces, and capacities. The software allows the creation of scorecards and setting goals, facilitating performance tracking in a compact view. A unique feature of Power BI is its ability to explore networks based on categorical data, offering customization options, support for image insertion, and multi-touch device functionality.

Unique Features of Power BI

AI-powered Insights: Power BI leverages artificial intelligence to provide automatic insights and analysis of data, uncovering hidden patterns, trends, and outliers. It helps users gain valuable and actionable insights without extensive manual exploration.

IBM Cognos Analytics

IBM Cognos Analytics stands out as an AI-powered BI solution that excels in reliable data preparation and reporting. This all-in-one platform seamlessly connects with your data, empowering you to generate visually appealing and user-friendly visualizations while predicting future business outcomes. With its advanced reporting functionalities, it caters to the needs of both small and large businesses.

One of the key strengths of IBM Cognos Analytics lies in its ability to automatically create interactive visualizations from your data, offering a comprehensive online library for immediate use. Additionally, it provides recommendations for visualizations that best illustrate your points, ensuring impactful communication of insights.

Unique features of IBM Cognos Analytics

- Self-service analytics empower users to explore and analyze data independently
- An AI assistant to assist in streamlining workflows
- Convenience in creating dashboards using mobile devices
- Automatic recommendation of charts, making it easier to choose the most effective visual representation

Streamlit

Streamlit is an open-source Python framework designed for Machine Learning and Data Science practitioners. It offers a streamlined approach to building interactive apps and dashboards without the need for a separate front-end framework. With Streamlit, users can transform their Python programs into engaging dashboards that incorporate real-time analytics and machine learning models.

The framework provides support for multiple charting libraries, such as Pyplot, Seaborn, Altair, Plotly, Bokeh, PyDeck, and more. These libraries come with comprehensive documentation, enabling Python programmers to easily create visually appealing applications. Streamlit's APIs are minimalistic, making it accessible even for novice Python programmers without specialized front-end programming skills.

Unique Features of Streamlit

- Design Flexibility: Streamlit offers great design flexibility, allowing individuals with basic Python programming skills to create customized dashboards quickly and easily.
- Rapid Application Development: With Streamlit, the application development process is accelerated, empowering users to build interactive dashboards swiftly.

Self-Service Data Visualization: Empowering with User-Friendly Tools

Self-service data visualization has become a crucial aspect of modern business operations, and the market offers various tools to make it a practical reality. Organizations no longer want to restrict their creativity when presenting data and building interactive dashboards and reports. Whether it is for new product launches, market analysis, competitor insights, research information, risk analysis, financial positions, or any other analytics, self-service is now a requirement across multiple functions such as sales, finance, marketing, supply chain, logistics, manufacturing, human resources, support, and information technology.

Every department seeks to gain tactical or strategic insights from data through user-friendly reports and visually appealing dashboards.

In general, self-service refers to providing non-technical end-users with tools to create reports and dashboards without the need for coding or technical expertise. The level of self-service can vary depending on the simplicity of creating the final dashboard or report. The easier the task, the higher the degree of self-service achieved. By promoting self-service, organizations can shift their focus from intricate data warehousing, BI tools, or data analytics methodologies to domain-specific knowledge and business requirements. While self-service may sound straightforward, it requires proper planning and implementation of people, processes, and tools to make it a success.

Considerations for organizations transitioning to self-service

- Business users need to understand the transformed or enriched data.
  - Business users may find it challenging to comprehend raw data in its crude form (such as binaries). Therefore, understanding the data after it has been transformed and enriched in a format that business users can easily interpret is essential.
  - Business users do not necessarily need to understand the complexities of raw data to enrich data transformation, as this is a technical function that specialized teams handle.
- Business users' level of analytics capability:
  - It is crucial to assess whether business users possess knowledge of SQL and commonly used office tools such as Excel.
  - Understanding statistics and aggregations can significantly enhance the effectiveness of self-service data visualization.
- The dynamic nature of reports and dashboards:
  - If reports and dashboards have standard formats with minimal changes required, the need for self-service may be lower.

- Self-service becomes highly advantageous when there is a demand for creative ad-hoc reporting and data exploration.

Steps to achieve self-service

- Establish a data governance framework: Set up a structured process to manage data quality, security, and compliance. Define roles and responsibilities for data access and ensure proper data governance practices are in place.
- Implement a data integration strategy: Connect and integrate data from various sources, both internal and external, to create a unified view of the information. This may involve data extraction, transformation, and loading (ETL) processes to ensure data consistency and reliability.
- Create a centralized data repository: Set up a data warehouse or data lake to store and organize the collected data in a structured and accessible format. Design data models that support efficient data retrieval and analysis.
- Develop user-friendly data visualization tools: Select and deploy intuitive self-service data visualization tools that enable users without technical expertise to create meaningful reports and interactive dashboards. Ensure these tools offer a wide range of visualization options and are easy to use.
- Provide training and support: Conduct training sessions to educate users on data visualization best practices and the effective use of self-service tools. Offer ongoing support and assistance to help users overcome any challenges they may encounter.
- Foster a data-driven culture: Encourage a culture of data-driven decision-making within the organization. Promote the use of self-service data visualization tools as a means to empower individuals to explore data, gain insights, and make informed decisions.
- Continuously iterate and improve: Regularly evaluate the effectiveness of the self-service data visualization initiative. Seek feedback from users

and identify areas for improvement. Make necessary adjustments to the data infrastructure, tools, and training to enhance the self-service capabilities over time.
- Leverage generative AI like ChatGPT: Integrate generative AI tools into the self-service data visualization environment to assist users in generating insightful visualizations, providing real-time recommendations, and enhancing the overall user experience.
- Organizations can establish a self-service data visualization environment that enables users to independently explore and analyze data, leading to more informed decision-making and improved business outcomes.

By following these steps and considering the necessary factors, organizations can successfully transition to self-service data visualization and empower their teams to gain actionable insights from data in a user-friendly manner.

Exercise
Selecting the Appropriate Visualization Tool
Objective:

The objective of this task is to engage in a critical evaluation process for selecting an appropriate data visualization tool for a given scenario. This task focuses on understanding and applying various factors that influence the selection of visualization tools, including deployment environment, customization, software type, data integration and refresh capabilities, and real-time analytics provision.

Scenario:

"HealthTrack9to5 Inc.," a healthcare analytics company, wants to adopt a new data visualization tool to analyze patient data more effectively. This tool will help them identify trends in patient health outcomes, optimize treatment plans, and forecast healthcare demands. The company deals with sensitive health data, requiring strict compliance with healthcare regulations. Their data is stored in multiple formats and locations, and they need to be able to update and analyze data in real time to respond quickly to emerging health crises.

Task Instructions:

1. Research and Selection: Research and select three data visualization tools that you believe could meet HealthTrack's needs. At least one tool should be an in-house server application, and one should be a cloud application. The selection should include both open-source and commercial software options.
2. Evaluation Criteria Development: Based on the factors provided (in-house server vs. cloud applications, degree of customization, open source vs. commercial software, data integration capability, data refresh capability, and provision for real-time analytics), you will develop a set of evaluation criteria to assess the suitability of each tool for HealthTrack.
3. Analysis and Recommendation: You will analyze each selected tool against the developed criteria, highlighting the strengths and weaknesses of each option in the context of HealthTrack's scenario. You should consider how each tool's features and limitations align with the company's requirements, especially regarding data security, integration, and real-time analytics.
4. Final Recommendation: Based on your analysis, you will make a final recommendation on which tool HealthTrack should adopt. You should justify the choice by discussing how this tool best aligns with the company's specific needs, considering all the factors influencing the selection.

Deliverable:

Prepare a report containing the following:

- A brief overview of the three selected data visualization tools.
- The set of evaluation criteria was developed based on the influencing factors.
- An analysis of each tool against the criteria, including pros and cons.
- A final recommendation with justification based on the analysis.

Leveraging External Resources for Informed Decision-Making:

This exercise provides a valuable opportunity to engage in a critical evaluation process for selecting the most appropriate data visualization tool for a given scenario. By researching and selecting three different tools, developing evaluation criteria, analyzing each tool against the criteria, and making a final recommendation, you will gain insights into the complex decision-making involved in choosing the right tool for the job.

As you navigate through this exercise, remember to leverage external resources such as Google or generative AI tools to gather additional insights and information. These resources can provide valuable assistance in understanding the capabilities and limitations of each tool, ensuring a well-informed decision-making process.

Ultimately, the exercise aims to enhance your ability to assess and select data visualization tools effectively, considering various factors such as deployment environment, customization options, data integration capabilities, and compliance requirements. By completing this exercise, you will be better equipped to make informed decisions when faced with similar challenges in real-world scenarios.

CASE STUDY: UNVEILING INSIGHTS FROM MUSIC SALES DATA WITH GENERATIVEAI'S GUIDANCE

Objective

Embark on your final project to apply the concepts acquired in this book with the assistance of ChatGPT. This case study will guide you through the process of analyzing music sales data stored in a MySQL database, empowering you to refine your visualization skills and derive actionable insights to drive business decisions.

Scenario

As a data analyst at a digital media company, you have been tasked with optimizing marketing and sales strategies using music sales data with the aid of ChatGPT. Armed with insights from "DEMYSTIFYING BUSINESS DATA VISUALIZATION," your journey begins as you explore the Chinook database—a repository teeming with media-related data sourced from a real iTunes Library. Within this database lies a wealth of untapped information. Utilize SQL queries to meticulously extract valuable insights and harness the power of Tableau to craft compelling visualizations that illuminate pathways for informed decision-making. Note that while the Chinook database contains authentic media-related data, customer and employee information is fictitious, ensuring confidentiality. Additionally, sales data is auto-generated using randomized information spanning four years. Detailed instructions below will guide you in leveraging your own iTunes Library to generate the necessary SQL scripts for analysis.

Enhancing Learning: Unlocking the Power of GenerativeAI

ChatGPT serves as a valuable resource throughout this case study, offering real-time assistance and guidance to enhance your learning experience. By leveraging the capabilities of Generative AI tools such as ChatGPT or Gemini, you can overcome challenges, receive SQL query suggestions, and address complex queries efficiently. This interactive learning approach fosters a deeper understanding of data analysis techniques and facilitates a more comprehensive exploration of the Chinook database. Ultimately, integrating ChatGPT into your workflow enhances your analytical skills, accelerates your learning curve, and enables you to derive richer insights from your data.

Chapter Integration

This case study seamlessly integrates the knowledge acquired from various chapters of "DEMYSTIFYING BUSINESS DATA VISUALIZATION" to offer you a comprehensive hands-on experience:

- Chapter 1: Understand the evolution of data visualization and sidestep common pitfalls.
- Chapter 2: Apply principles of visual perception to design effective visualizations.
- Chapter 3: Harness the power of visualization in analytics for exploratory analysis and goal-driven insights.

CASE STUDY: Unveiling Insights from Music Sales Data with GenerativeAI's Guidance

- Chapter 4: Navigate the visualization project lifecycle, from scoping to audience-focused communication.
- Chapter 5: Explore modern tools for data visualization and select the right tool for the task.

Steps

1. Download the Chinook Database
   a. Access the Chinook database from https://github.com/lerocha/chinook-database.
   b. Review the "README" section to understand the data model and other information provided on the dataset.

2. Set up the Chinook Database:
   a. Import the Chinook database into MySQL by establishing a new database and importing the SQL file containing the Chinook schema and data.
   b. Using ChatGPT: If you encounter any difficulties during the setup process, you can ask ChatGPT for assistance. For example:
      i. "Can you provide step-by-step instructions on how to import a MySQL database?"
      ii. "How can I import the Chinook database into MySQL?"

3. Explore the Database Tables:
   a. Utilize SQL queries to navigate the tables within the Chinook database.
   b. Using ChatGPT: If you are unsure about how to navigate the tables or need assistance with specific SQL queries, ChatGPT can help. For example:
      i. "Can you provide SQL queries to display the first few rows of each table in the Chinook database?"
      ii. "How can I retrieve information about the structure of a specific table in MySQL?"

4. Identify Key Insights:
   a. Employ principles from Chapter 3 to discern key metrics and insights from the Chinook database.
   b. Using ChatGPT: If you need assistance in identifying key insights or formulating SQL queries to extract specific metrics, ChatGPT can assist. For example:
      i. "What SQL queries can I use to calculate the total revenue generated by each track in the Chinook database?"
      ii. "How can I identify the top-selling artists in the Chinook database using SQL?"

5. Write SQL Queries:
   a. Craft SQL queries to extract desired insights from the Chinook database, drawing upon techniques elucidated in Chapter 4.
   b. Using ChatGPT: If you encounter challenges in crafting SQL queries or need assistance with complex queries, ChatGPT is available to help. For example:
      i. "ChatGPT, what SQL queries can I use to identify the top 10 highest-spending customers in the Chinook database?"
      ii. "How can I create a SQL query to calculate the total revenue generated by each genre in the Chinook database?"
      iii. "Can you provide a SQL query to find the average purchase amount per customer in the Chinook database?"
      iv. "How can I join the 'Customers' and 'Invoices' tables to retrieve customer information along with their corresponding invoice details?"
      v. "ChatGPT, please suggest a SQL query to identify tracks that have been purchased but not played in the Chinook database."
      vi. "What SQL query should I use to calculate the total sales revenue for each month in the Chinook database?"

vii. "ChatGPT, how can I write a SQL query to determine the total number of customers who have made purchases in each country in the Chinook database?"

viii. "Can you provide SQL queries to calculate the total sales revenue for each employee in the Chinook database?"

ix. "How can I create a SQL query to identify customers who have purchased a specific genre of music multiple times in the Chinook database?"

x. "ChatGPT, what SQL queries can I use to analyze the correlation between the length of a track and its popularity, measured by the number of times it has been purchased?"

xi. "ChatGPT, I need assistance with a complex SQL query. Can you provide a query to calculate the total sales amount for each customer, along with the average sale amount and the number of purchases made by each customer? Below are the sample table structures:

Sales Table:

sale_id	customer_id	product_id	sale_amount
1	101	201	50.00
2	102	202	75.00
3	103	203	30.00
4	104	204	45.00
5	105	205	60.00

Customers Table:

```
----------------------------------------
| customer_id | name | country |
----------------------------------------
| 101 | John | USA |
| 102 | Mary | Canada |
| 103 | Alice | USA |
| 104 | Bob | UK |
| 105 | Emma | France |
----------------------------------------"
```

6. Apply Structured Analysis and Formulate Recommendations:
   a. Utilize the insights derived from SQL queries to generate recommendations for optimizing marketing and sales strategies.
   b. Create a detailed business analysis document incorporating tasks from Chapter 4.
      i. Business Requirement: Define the overarching business need for optimizing marketing and sales strategies using music sales data.
      ii. SMART Goal: Establish specific, measurable, achievable, relevant, and time-bound goals for the project.
      iii. Scope of the Project: Outline the boundaries and objectives of the project, specifying what will and will not be included.
      iv. Audience: Identify the target audience for the analysis and ensure that insights are tailored to their needs.
      v. Assumptions: Document any assumptions made during the analysis process to provide context for the findings.

vi. Data Sources (Database): Specify the data sources used, including the Chinook database and any additional sources.

vii. High-Level Architecture: Provide an overview of the architecture required to support the analysis, including data pipelines and storage.

viii. Project Schedule: Develop a timeline for project milestones and deliverables to ensure timely completion.

ix. Project Team Structure: Define the roles and responsibilities of team members involved in the project.

x. KPI Design Document: Design key performance indicators (KPIs) to measure the success of marketing and sales strategies.

7. Generate Insights and Recommendations:
   a. Connect Tableau to the Chinook database and import pertinent tables.
   b. Create captivating visualizations in Tableau to effectively communicate insights, applying concepts from this book.
   c. Analyze visualizations to uncover patterns, trends, and correlations in the data, integrating knowledge gained throughout the book.
   d. Using ChatGPT: If you are unsure about how to create specific visualizations or need guidance on best practices, ChatGPT can provide assistance. For example:
      i. "Please provide steps to connect Tableau to MySQL?"
      ii. "What types of visualizations can I create in Tableau to represent the sales distribution across different genres in the Chinook database?"

Conclusion

Upon completion of this case study, you will emerge equipped with practical experience in applying concepts from "DEMYSTIFYING BUSINESS DATA VISUALIZATION" to real-world data analysis scenarios. You will adeptly navigate the visualization project lifecycle, select appropriate tools, and eloquently communicate insights to drive informed business decisions.

Additional Resources

- Access tutorials and documentation for MySQL, Tableau, and other pertinent tools, including Generative AI tools such as ChatGPT and Gemini, to support further learning.
- Encourage exploration of additional datasets and continued practice of data visualization skills independently.

CONCLUSION

In this book, we have explored the vast and evolving field of data visualization. We began by delving into the history and evolution of data visualization and understanding how it has transformed in modern times with the advancements in technology. We discussed the importance of effective visualization and the pitfalls of poor visualization.

Next, we examined the principles of visual perception and how they form the foundation of successful data visualization. Understanding the role of human perception and the gestalt principles allowed us to build effective visualizations that communicate information clearly and intuitively. We explored the different elements and attributes that make up data visualizations and discussed the process of choosing the right visual representation for the data and the target audience.

Moving forward, we focused on the application of visualization in data science. We explored the role of visualization in exploratory data analysis, emphasizing the importance of visualizations in uncovering patterns, trends, and insights in data. We discussed various techniques for visualizing categorical data and highlighted the significance of setting SMART goals to guide the visualization process.

Shifting our attention to performance metrics, we explored the approaches and steps involved in visualizing performance metrics for businesses. From scoping the project to understanding data sources, acquiring data, defining business logic, and considering the audience, we provided a comprehensive guide for effectively visualizing performance metrics.

Lastly, we examined the modern tools available for data visualization. We discussed the factors to consider when selecting a visualization tool and provided an overview of various tools in the market. We also explored the concept of self-service data visualization, empowering users with the ability to create their own visualizations and gain insights from data without relying heavily on technical expertise.

In the final part of this journey, we applied the concepts learned in this book to a practical case study on music sales data. By leveraging the principles, techniques, and tools discussed, we explored the Chinook database with the aid of Generative AI tools. This hands-on experience enabled us to refine our visualization skills, extract actionable insights, and drive informed business decisions.

Throughout this book, we have emphasized the importance of data visualization as a powerful tool for understanding complex information and making informed decisions. By continuing to explore new techniques and pushing the boundaries of what is possible with data visualization, we can unlock the true potential of our data and drive meaningful insights.

With the knowledge gained from this book and the resources provided, we are confident that you are well-equipped to embark on your data visualization journey and make a meaningful impact in your field. Happy visualizing!

REFERENCES

1. The History and Evolution of SMART Goals:
   AchieveIt. (n.d.). The history and evolution of SMART goals. Retrieved from **https://www.achieveit.com/resources/blog/the-history-and-evolution-of-smart-goals**
2. The Dysfunctional Evolution of Goal Setting:
   Amabile, T. M., & Kramer, S. J. (2012). The dysfunctional evolution of goal setting. MIT Sloan Management Review, 53(3), 59–67. Retrieved from **https://sloanreview.mit.edu/article/the-dysfunctional-evolution-of-goal-setting-2/**
3. SMART Goals Template for Strategic and Data-Driven Managers:
   Northpass. (n.d.). SMART goals template for strategic and data-driven managers. Retrieved from **https://www.northpass.com/blog/smart-goals-template-for-strategic-and-data-driven-managers**
4. Bank Marketing Dataset:
   Moro, S., Cortez, P., & Rita, P. (2014). Bank marketing dataset. Retrieved from **https://archive.ics.uci.edu/ml/datasets/Bank+Marketing**
5. Hypotheses Development Example in Biology:
   Carleton College. (n.d.). Hypotheses development example in biology. Retrieved from **https://serc.carleton.edu/sp/cause/conjecture/examples/18163.html**

Made in the USA
Monee, IL
03 May 2026

49438946R00085